PROJECT MANAGEMENT
for the Technical Professional

PROJECT MANAGEMENT
for the Technical Professional

Michael Singer Dobson

PROJECT MANAGEMENT INSTITUTE

Library of Congress Cataloging-in-Publication Data

Dobson, Michael Singer.
    Project management for the technical professional / Michael Singer Dobson.
       p.   cm.
    Includes bibliographical references and index.
    ISBN: 1-880410-76-1
    1. Project management.   I. Title.

T56.8 .D63 2001
658.4'04 – – dc21   00-046449
                                       CIP

ISBN: 1-880410-76-1

Published by: Project Management Institute, Inc.
              Four Campus Boulevard
              Newtown Square, Pennsylvania 19073-3299 USA
              Phone +610-356-4600 or visit our website: www.pmi.org

PMI® books are available at special quantity discounts to use as premiums and sales promotions, or for use in corporate training programs, as well as other educational programs. For more information, please write to the Business Manager, PMI Publishing Division, Forty Colonial Square, Sylva, NC 28779 USA. Or contact your local bookstore.

The paper used in this book complies with the Permanent Paper Standard issued by the National Information Standards Organization (Z39.48—1984).

10 9 8 7 6 5 4 3 2 1

Dedication

Dedicated to my fellow project management trainers, friends,
and road warriors, including★:

Bob Bapes
Bill Capstack
Marshall Lee Dodd
Rosina Harter
Ted Leemann
Pat McWard
Kai Rambow
Richard Vail
Dain Zinn

for their advice, encouragement, mentoring, support, and feedback.

★but not limited to. …

Contents

All case studies in this book are based on real people and real situations experienced by or shared directly with the author. However, names and salient details have been changed to protect the innocent and guilty—and neutral—alike. Notes are included at the end of sections and chapters, and exercises are included in the chapters.

List of Figures ix
List of Case Studies/Sidebars x
SECTION ONE—INSIDE/OUT LEADERSHIP 1
  Chapter 1—On the Threshold of Advancement 3
    Transformation and Change 3
    What Is a Technical Professional? 3
    Managing Yourself to Manage Others 4
    Strategy and Self-Assessment 5
  Chapter 2—Knowing Thyself 7
    Action Planning for Success 7
  Chapter 3—Payoffs and Prices 17
    How Technical Professionals View Management 17
    Where You Stand Depends on Where You Sit 17
  Chapter 4—Management: It's Not Just a Job; It's a Career Change 27
    The Changing Skill Mix 27
    Management Surprises 30
SECTION TWO—THE ART, CRAFT, AND SCIENCE OF MANAGEMENT 35
  Chapter 5—The Mission of Management 37
    A Mission Statement for a Manager 37
    The Real World of Management and Supervision 37
    Styles of Supervision and Management 41
    Choosing Your Supervisory Style 45
  Chapter 6—Communications and Leadership 49
    Situation and Direction 49
    Communications 50
    How to Give and Get Feedback 54
    Listening ... and Being Quiet 55
    Communication and Technical Professionals 58
  Chapter 7—Management and Supervisory Skills 61
    The Work of Supervisors and Managers 61
    Delegation 61
    Recruiting and Staffing 65
    Training 68
    Motivation and Behavior Modification 68
    Discipline and Termination 73
    Conflict Management 74
    Legal and Regulatory Issues 76
    Finance and Budgeting 77
    Self-Development as a Manager 78
  Chapter 8—Alphabet Soup (or Management Initiatives for Quality) 81
    Management Philosophies 81

Management Fads—Threat or Menace? 81
Business Process Reengineering 83
Excellence Model (Peters/Waterman) 83
ISO-9000 84
Kaizen 86
Learning Organizations (Senge) 86
Management by Exception 86
Management by Objectives 87
Management by Wandering/Walking Around 88
Scientific Management 88
Self-Directed Work Teams and Other Teams 88
Statistical Process Control/Statistical Quality Control 89
Total Quality Management 90
Workforce 2000 92
Zero-Base Budgeting 94
What Makes These Methods Successful (or Not) 94

SECTION THREE—MANAGING TECHNICAL PROFESSIONALS **99**
  Chapter 9—TechnoCulture **101**
    Understanding Corporate Culture 101
    Characteristics of Technical Cultures 103
    Overcoming Change Resistance 105
    Modifying Organizational Culture 106
  Chapter 10—Teams and Structure **109**
    Organizational and Team Structures—Which Is Best for You? 109
    Individual-Oriented Workgroup Structure 113
    Specialist Group Structure 117
    Project Team Workgroup Structure 122
    Self-Directed Work Team Group Structure 125
    Tiger Teams and *Skunk Works*—A Special Structure 127
  Chapter 11—Power and People Issues **129**
    More Power! 129
    In-Demand Technical Professionals 133
    Difficult Technical Professionals and Other People 135
    Managing People Who Know More than You (or at Least Different Things) 136
    Managing Generation X 137
    How Managers Create Problem Employees—and How You Can Avoid It 139
  Chapter 12—Managing the Unofficial Organization **141**
    Office Politics and Newtonian Physics 141
    Managing Other Departments and People Who Don't Work for You 142
    Managing Unclear and Escalating Objectives 144

SECTION FOUR—MANAGING TECHNICAL PROJECTS **149**
  Chapter 13—Technical Project Management Issues **151**
    Technical Projects and the Industrial Revolution 151
    Characteristics of High-Technology Projects 151
    Limitations and Cautions in Using Project Management Tools 155
  Chapter 14—Organizational and Customer Issues in Technology Project Management **159**
    The Alchemical Mysteries 159
    The Priesthood of Project Managers 159
    "Tim (the Tool Man) Taylor"ism 160
    Between Scylla and Charybdis—The Challenge of Multiple Projects 161
  Conclusion **165**
  Bibliography **167**
  Index **171**

List of Figures

Figure 1 Inside/Out Supervision 1
Figure 2 The Pareto Principle 25
Figure 3 Balancing Technical and Management Skills 29
Figure 4 The McKinsey 7-S Framework 50
Figure 5 The Transmission Model of Communication 51
Figure 6 Maslow's Hierarchy of Needs 72
Figure 7 SPC Control Chart 90
Figure 8 The Three Foundations of TQM 92
Figure 9 Organizational Change Model 106
Figure 10 Determining Organizational Structure 110
Figure 11 Innovation Model for Leadership 126
Figure 12 Morale Killers in the Workplace 140

List of Case Studies/Sidebars

Case Study 1—Is It Right for You? 4
Case Study 2—Managers? We Don't Need No Stinkin' Managers! 11
How to Become a Manager 28
The Godzilla Principle 30
Case Study 3—You Knew That the Job Was Dangerous When You Took It 31
Case Study 4—B-O-S-S Spelled Backwards Is Double-S-O-B 38
Case Study 5—Can't Live With Them, Can't Kill Them 43
Case Study 6—"Paranoia Strikes Deep (into Your Heart It Will Creep)" 52
Rules for Effective Delegation 62
Six Steps for Better Hiring 66
Case Study 7—Performance Is Punished 70
Case Study 8—Failure Is Rewarded 70
Case Study 9—Performance Doesn't Matter 71
Nine Steps to Proper Discipline 74
Case Study 10—People Unclear on the Concept I 77
Reengineering Fundamentals 84
Eight Elements of the Excellent Company 85
The Five Disciplines 87
The Seven Basic Tools of SPC 91
Deming's Fourteen Points 93
Crosby's Absolutes of Quality Management 93
Case Study 11—People Unclear on the Concept II 95
Glossary of TechnoCulture Terms 102
How to Give Out Great Job Assignments 114
Using Teamwork with Individual Work 116
Thirteen Characteristics of Effective Work Teams 117
The Development Life Cycle of a Team (Tuckman Model) 118
Why Some Projects Fail ... and Others Succeed 122
The Four R's of Power 130
Example—Positive and Negative Workplace Characteristics 135
Case Study 12—Baby Killing 162–163

Section One
INSIDE/OUT LEADERSHIP

As Randy Newman wrote (and Frank Sinatra sang), "It's lonely at the top." As a technical professional advancing into a leadership role, or as a manager of technical professionals—whether or not you have a technical background in the same field—you face significant challenges and possess exciting opportunities.

While experts have different ideas about what constitutes effective leadership and how to be an effective leader, they tend to agree on one essential element: unless you control yourself, you will be ineffective at controlling others.

Effective leadership starts within. Only by complete and honest self-assessment can you develop the appropriate action plan and direction that enables you to grow and achieve. Only by identifying your payoffs and your goals can you maximize your productivity and achievement. Through a combination of exercises and description, the material in this section is designed to help you begin your journey.

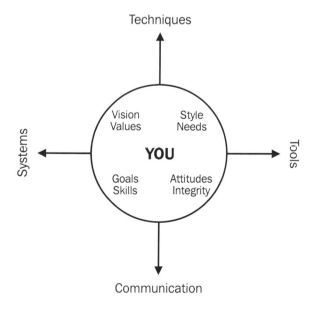

Figure 1 Inside/Out Supervision

Chapter 1
On the Threshold of Advancement

Transformation and Change

Entering management isn't a promotion—it's a career change. From an orientation around things, ideas, and issues to a new focus on people, personalities, and politics, from being self-directed to having to work through other people, from caring only about the work product to caring about company financial issues, managers of all stripes find that making the transition is a wrenching experience, both in terms of workload and in terms of emotional whiplash.

For no group is the transition quite as disruptive as for the technical professional who has suddenly been moved into a leadership role. While it's a gross and unfair generalization to link technical professionals with pocket-protector, propeller beanie-wearing, Dilbert-loving, Grade-A nerds and geeks, certainly many of the people who entered technical positions in the first place did so because of a love of the work itself. Instead of simply becoming more connected with the work at a higher level, technical professionals in management ranks find themselves slipping away from some of their original sources of career satisfaction.

What Is a Technical Professional?

For our purpose, *technical professional* refers to anyone who needs an advanced skill set to perform the tasks and projects inherent in a particular job. They include:
- computer/information technology professionals
- engineers of all varieties
- design professionals
- architects
- medical professionals (physicians and others)
- and many more.

These occupations frequently require specific educational backgrounds, and there are often specific college degrees in those topics (whether or not all members of the profession have them or need them). Technical fields tend to require logical and factual thinking. There are right and wrong answers available for many of the problems faced. The work is often project oriented (1).

Case Study 1

Is It Right for You?

John joined RST Associates as a draftsman when the company still consisted of five people in a third-floor walk-up office—and then the company caught fire. In five years it went from sales of under $50,000 to over $30 million, and John grew with it. At twenty-eight years old, he was making over $100,000 per year as vice president of logistics in one of the fastest-growing companies in America. He had a big office, a company car, over forty staff members, a budget totaling in the millions, and all the trappings of success.

He also had an ulcer, a broken marriage, an eighty-hour work week, and troubled sleep. Every morning he woke up sweating, with feelings of dread about going to work. But this was *success*, he thought.

Finally, John realized the truth. He loved the work but hated being a manager. So he decided to become truly successful. He negotiated a demotion and a $60,000 pay cut, and returned to being a draftsman.

His ulcer cleared up, he reconciled with his spouse, and now he can sleep at night. Management isn't for everybody, and success is something you must self-measure.

Managing Yourself to Manage Others

This book addresses these core issues, both emotional and procedural, to help technical professionals cope with the transition to their leadership role, and to learn how to connect emotionally with the real payoffs that exist.

To manage others successfully, you must first manage yourself. That means analyzing your strengths and weaknesses, realizing that what were once strengths when you were a technical professional can sometimes become weaknesses as a manager.

Strengths and weaknesses don't only have to do with your skills, abilities, and intelligence; they also have to do with your personal commitment. Desire is a qualification for management: if you don't want to do something, then you aren't likely to do it well, regardless of your intelligence or inherent ability. If you want to do something, then your desire tends to make you more successful at it. The core aptitude for management success, then, becomes your desire for your new role—what politicians call the "fire in the belly." Sometimes, very talented people discover that management is not the right choice for them. If that turns out to be the case for you, it's important to know it so that you can make career decisions not based on what you *ought* to do, but instead on the core values and aptitudes that you truly possess. Nothing in the workplace is sadder than someone who has become *Peter Principled*: promoted to the level of his own incompetence.

Strategy and Self-Assessment

Take the time to complete the exercises and self-assessments in this book. By doing so, you will end with an action plan that will help you face the challenges ahead with success and integrity—remembering that success must be self-measured.

Consider your goals and overall career strategy. Successful careers do not happen by accident. Make a plan to get what you want.

Determine that you will treat becoming an effective leader, supervisor, and manager with the same dedication and zeal that you used to develop your competence in your current field.

Set long-term goals and action plans, because most of the important changes you may need to make take time and effort.

Start today.

Notes

1. A *project* is distinct from *work* in that a project ends and has a measurable output. See Dobson 1996 and 1999b.

Chapter 2
Knowing Thyself

Action Planning for Success

As a technical professional in a leadership role, whether your transition is recent or has been going on for some time, you need to evaluate your strengths and weaknesses in order to develop a personal action plan for success.

In the next several pages, you'll complete a self-assessment exercise to profile how you fit or don't fit some of the traditional characteristics associated with the technical professional. Because we are all different and individual, you will find that you relate in some ways and not in others.

Following the exercise, you'll read description and commentary on these characteristics, showing how they may affect your success and achievement in a leadership role. You'll learn more detail about each area as you continue to read. As you continue through this book, you'll explore areas in more detail so that you can develop success strategies to make the most of your situation.

While the goal of this book is to help you be successful in your leadership role, remember that one option you have is to elect not to be a manager or leader at all. Don't let other people set your definition of success and achievement; you can't be successful at someone else's goal if it is not one that you share.

Let's start by comparing your personality, strengths, weaknesses, and outlook to that of the traditional, or stereotypical, technical professional.

Exercise 1

Characteristics of the Technical Professional

Certain characteristics form a stereotype of the *technical professional*. As with all stereotypes, individuals who are technical professionals may share some, but likely do not share all, of those characteristics. In this exercise, rate to what degree you feel each characteristic describes you. It's important to remember that there are neither right nor wrong answers in this exercise.

Characteristic	STRONGLY DESCRIBES		SOMEWHAT DESCRIBES		NOT AT ALL
1. Values logic over emotions	5	4	3	2	1
2. More loyal to the profession than to the organization	5	4	3	2	1
3. Believes ideas and the work are more important than people	5	4	3	2	1
4. Has limited people skills	5	4	3	2	1
5. Doesn't care very much about people and their feelings	5	4	3	2	1
6. Disdains *office politics* as a waste of time	5	4	3	2	1
7. Sets own standards for quality rather than rely on others' standards	5	4	3	2	1
8. Believes the primary purpose of the organization is—or ought to be— to do quality work	5	4	3	2	1
9. Prefers to do the work personally because she can do it faster and better	5	4	3	2	1
10. Values solving a problem as a key job satisfier	5	4	3	2	1
11. Strongly prefers and needs independent work	5	4	3	2	1
12. Always strives for a *perfect* outcome rather than one that is merely *acceptable*	5	4	3	2	1
13. Spends personal time regularly studying his field of interest	5	4	3	2	1
14. Resists standards set by others unless they are equally technically competent	5	4	3	2	1
15. Believes emotions have little legitimate role in technical decisions	5	4	3	2	1
16. Doesn't generally consider others' feelings in doing the right things	5	4	3	2	1
17. Believes that being right is more important than building relationships	5	4	3	2	1
18. Often feels that others, especially in management, don't care as much about quality	5	4	3	2	1
19. Rates herself compared to others based primarily on technical knowledge	5	4	3	2	1
20. Is not known for personal fashion sense	5	4	3	2	1

21. Believes himself to be more competent and intelligent than most others	5	4	3	2	1
22. Is primarily a specialist, not a generalist	5	4	3	2	1
23. Has unusual hobbies or interests that are pursued with great passion	5	4	3	2	1
24. Believes authority and respect must be earned by those in power, not automatically assumed	5	4	3	2	1
25. Feels socially awkward, an *outsider*	5	4	3	2	1

Debrief of Exercise 1

Because this is a profile rather than a test, there is no official score, nor is it important as such whether you fit elements of the technical professional stereotype.

What is important is that you evaluate yourself and your personal characteristics in light of your career and professional goals. While some of the characteristics may be considered *good* and others *bad*, the reality is that most of these characteristics are situational: useful and positive (or at least neutral) in some situations, disadvantageous in other situations.

To be successful in a leadership role, you are looking for a quality called "style flexibility," which allows you to be functional and effective in a wide range of situations and with a wide range of people. Your goal isn't to get a personality transplant or to reject parts of who you are and have been; rather, it is to develop improved functionality in the leadership role that you have chosen.

Let's look at the individual characteristics in more detail.

1. Values logic over emotions. The appreciation for rational thought is a classic characteristic associated with the technical professional, and, of course, logic is a valuable tool. It would clearly be a bad idea to ignore or put aside logic and rationality, but it is a good idea to realize that nonlogical thinking isn't the same as irrational thinking. Emotions and values have a large impact on organizational decisions, and they are essential in understanding human interaction. Your goal should be to add more appreciation for nonrational thought to your arsenal. After all, as the saying goes, "When the only tool you have is a hammer, all problems look like nails."

2. More loyal to the profession than to the organization. Loyalty to the profession describes the attitude of a technical professional to her work. For example, a computer specialist may be primarily concerned with computer-based solutions, rather than with taking a wider organizational perspective. If what is best for the organization is to ignore or downplay the importance of the technical field, then this characteristic may provide difficulty to the technical professional. As a manager, you are expected to take an organizational perspective at all times, even when it is to the detriment of your department or your profession.

3. Believes ideas and the work are more important than people. It's not that you necessarily believe that people are unimportant, but that the work and quality of ideas come first. People may not like you for being right, but what difference should that make? As a manager, you quickly discover that people relationships are essential for making ideas into reality: if people don't like you, it may not be nearly enough that you are right.

4. Has limited people skills. The cliché is that technical professionals are devoid of people skills, often awkward or unable to deal with people in an effective way. This goes along with the idea that technical professionals are also introverts. Of course, being an introvert has little to do with one's skill in people relationships. The difference is not in whether you like or dislike people, but in where you get your energy. According to Myers-Briggs Type Indicator experts David Keirsey and Marilyn Bates, "Introverts enjoy interacting with others, but it drains their energy in a way not experienced by extraverts. Introverts need to find quiet places and solitary activities to recharge, while these activities exhaust the extravert" (1984, 15). Because people tire the introvert, the introvert may not work as hard to acquire people skills, but there is nothing about introversion per se that produces poor people skills.

5. Doesn't care very much about people and their feelings. This is a separate characteristic from poor people skills or introversion. In fact, an extrovert can dislike and devalue people; the extrovert merely needs people around him as a source of energy. You don't actually have to care about people for their own sakes—although it's clearly valuable if you do—but you must at a minimum be able to show caring and respect to be successful in any leadership role.

6. Disdains office politics as a waste of time. Learning how to use office politics is of essential importance to getting things done on a daily basis. Much of what people refer to as *office politics* is actually bad office politics. No matter what, you must accept the reality that office politics exists in any organization that employs three or more people, and that dealing with political issues is an unavoidable part of your job. Having a positive attitude about it is critical, given the reality that people tend to do well what they value and not well what they don't value.

7. Sets own standards for quality rather than rely on others' standards. Technical professionals tend to care about their professions—that's why they worked so hard to master their skills. As a result, there is a tendency to believe that your quality standards are often higher and certainly more exacting than the standards of others—the user population—who may not understand the nature of what you do. The limiting aspect of this idea is that in an organization, others' standards are often the ones by which your work is judged. It's important to understand that quality is a customer-centered concept. Quality expert Ralph Berkowitz asks:

> What is quality? Is it defect free products and services; total attention to service; a customer service agent that is knowledgeable, responsive, and capable of dealing with the buyer; price; or well designed and easy to use products? The answer to these questions is … YES! … What the customer wants, their overriding focus, is to have their EXPECTATIONS met (and exceeded if possible) [1994, 6].

8. Believes the primary purpose of the organization is to do quality work. Organizations are always run for multiple purposes. While you may not always like or agree with those purposes, you need to accept their reality and understand that certain strategic decisions follow from them. In the real world, organizations often have one of three driving forces: quality/product, finance, or marketing/sales. You'll notice that certain vice presidents tend to have more power and authority than others, and that may give you the tipoff about your own organization. Organizations can be very successful using any of the three techniques, but it's important that you know in advance how your organization is organized.

9. Prefers to do the work personally because she can do it faster and better. The difficulty here is that it is often true that you can do it faster and better. Nevertheless, it's essential

---

Case Study 2

Managers? We Don't Need No Stinkin' Managers!

It was only Susan's first week as the new section head in the information technology group. She expected some challenges and people problems, but she was shocked at the basic negativity directed at the whole idea and concept of management.

The worst one was Harry, who actually said, with a contemptuous sneer in his voice, "I don't see how you provide any value added to my work, so as far as I'm concerned, I don't have a manager."

Susan didn't have an answer. Instinctively, she knew she had a purpose and a role, but it was one that she had trouble articulating.

Managers and management do add value to the work that's done. Remember that none of the work is done as an end in itself; work is always done as a means to an end. Make sure that you understand the organizational mission and direction, and the role that you play in its achievement. Perhaps you won't convince the Harrys of this world, but you will at least know why you are there.

---

to delegate for two reasons: 1) to make time for yourself to do those things that only you can do, and 2) to train others to improve their own skills. Watch for a common failing of new managers who are insecure in their new responsibilities. Instead of doing what they should be doing, they shoulder their own staff out of the way in order to do the work they understand. This isn't being quality driven; it's failing to understand your new role.

10. Values solving a problem as a key job satisfier. Technical work—and management work as well—often consists of identifying and solving problems. Solving problems is productive, because when a problem is solved, that particular problem is no longer an issue. Problem solving is rewarding, both professionally and emotionally, because you get the feeling of success and achievement. However, as a manager, you must adapt in two ways: 1) realize that many of your most important problems can't be solved, only managed (*Example*: If you don't have enough staff to do the work, will you get more, or will you have to figure how to cope with what you've got?); 2) realize that there is often no single perfect solution to the problems you face. You know you're a real manager when you realize that you're not so much being paid for making good decisions as you are for being the person who chooses when all the alternatives are stinky and unpleasant.

11. Strongly prefers and needs independent work. A desire to do independent work is associated with the introversion that is often characteristic of the technical professional. Unfortunately, it's not a characteristic of management as a profession. In addition, in a world in which teams and team orientation are becoming more and more part of the corporate environment, it's something not always available for technical professionals themselves!

12. Always strives for a perfect outcome rather than one that is merely acceptable. There is an essential danger in perfectionism: it runs the risk of making *perfect* the enemy of *good*. Even with a strong focus on quality, you must always start your projects and your work by determining the *good-enough* point. That doesn't mean that you'll necessarily stay there. There's often value in exceeding good enough. First, it's hard to exceed good enough when you don't know where that point is. Second, exceeding good enough has a value and a cost associated with the value, if only the value of the work you could have done instead with the time and resources (1). In most work, there is a breakeven point at which further investment is not profitable or desirable. The failure to recognize this is the source of much criticism of technical professionals.

13. Spends personal time regularly studying his field of interest. This is clearly a valuable and positive characteristic. Technical professionals tend naturally to understand Stephen Covey's "Sharpen the Saw" concept: "Education—continuing education, continually honing and expanding the mind—is vital mental renewal" (1989, 295). What is important now is to expand the range of your study. By reading this book, you are stretching your skills in new areas—areas in which you may not have received formal education or training. As Covey also says:

> It is extremely valuable to train the mind to stand apart and examine its own program. That, to me, is the definition of a liberal education—the ability to examine the programs of life against larger questions and purposes and other paradigms. Training, without such education, narrows and closes the mind so that the assumptions underlying the training are never examined (1989, 295).

14. Resists standards set by others unless they are equally technically competent. You will probably have noticed a tendency in some technical professionals to judge—and judge harshly—the knowledge and skill of their customers, both internal and external. It's essential to remember that there is no obligation for customers to be competent in building the products and services that they want and need. In fact, their lack of competence in those areas keeps you employed. Further, there are many products and services that you need that you don't have the competence to perform personally—yet you do know one thing: what you need and want. In an organization, the standards are set for your work based on customer needs and desires, and that is the way it should be.

15. Believes emotions have little legitimate role in technical decisions. How you *feel* about the Law of Gravity or whether you think it's *fair* that an innocent person will probably die if she falls off a tall building has very little to do with the reality of the situation (2). Many technical issues are factual in nature, and emotional reactions to those decisions are essentially irrelevant. Combined with the logic/rationality emphasis of the technical professional, this leads to a general rule that emotions have little legitimate place in the technical decision process. However, emotions are as real as the Law of Gravity, and must be recognized and acknowledged. It's also important to be aware that people who disdain emotions in others often have strong emotions themselves—although they often express their emotion by claiming *facts* that may not be in evidence.

16. Doesn't generally consider others' feelings in doing the right things. In a study of star performers at Bell Labs, researchers discovered that there was little innate IQ difference in the abilities of the star performers and the average to below-average performers. The difference was their command of interpersonal and emotional strategies to work with others and to recognize their emotions. One of the most important turned out to be a rapport with a network of key people (Goleman 1995, 162). In other words, feelings are not an optional ingredient in achieving success.

17. Believes that being right is more important than building relationships. The reality, again, is that your relationships determine whether your *rightness* will turn into action. "Just because people work together day to day," emotional intelligence expert Daniel Goleman notes, "they will not necessarily trust each other with sensitive information … nor turn to them in crisis. … The stars of an organization are often those who have thick connections on all networks, whether communications, expertise, or trust" (1995, 162).

18. Often feels that others, especially in management, don't care as much about quality. This gets back to the definition of quality itself. Quality expert Philip Crosby defines it as "conformance to requirements" and points out that the key element is defining the requirements. "If a Cadillac conforms to all the requirements of a Cadillac, then it is a quality car. If a Pinto conforms to all the requirements of a Pinto, then it is a quality car" (1980, 15). The critical question then becomes: Who decides the requirements? Ultimately, it is the customer, and those requirements are translated back through the marketing and management chain into the work requirements for the technical professional. If those requirements are badly done, then the product or service will naturally have poor quality. On the other hand, there are often elements that the technical professional values that are not necessarily valued by the customer, and that's where the problem enters. If the code is not *elegant*, yet it fully satisfies requirements, management may want to stop the project, but the technical professional still sees substantial room for improvement. In your leadership role, you need to focus on customer-centered quality in making these decisions.

19. Rates himself compared to others based primarily on technical knowledge. "Dilbert" creator Scott Adams observes:

> Nothing is more threatening to the [technical professional] than the suggestion somebody has more technical skill. … When [a technical professional] says that something can't be done … some clever normal people have learned to glance at the [technical professional] with a look of compassion and pity and say something along these lines: "I'll ask Bob to figure it out. He knows how to solve difficult technical problems" (1996, 191).

One of the key strategies for success in a leadership role over technical professionals is mastering the art of praise, including recognizing when others possess more skill, knowledge, or ability in certain areas than you do—in other words, managing your ego effectively.

20. Not known for personal fashion sense. Of course, this is one of the most common clichés about technical professionals. Scott Adams observes, "Clothes are the lowest priority for [a technical professional], assuming the basic thresholds for temperature and decency have been satisfied"(1996, 176). To achieve or go further in a leadership role, you must make sure that you have mastered at least the basics of professional dress. Communications experts Barbara Pachter and Marjorie Brody put it this way:

> If you want to play the game, you have to wear the uniform. … There are no hard-and-fast rules for corporate dressing. The best guideline is to follow the example of upper management. (Make sure the upper management person you choose is a good role model.) That doesn't mean you have to look like a clone of your boss. … Even if the dress code in your organization tends to be casual, it's still important to keep your look polished, pulled together, and professional (1995, 106).

21. Believes herself to be more competent and intelligent than others. It may well be true that you are more competent and intelligent than others in your organization or on your team, but showing it in your attitude and behavior is a quick route to trouble. In Myers-Briggs Type Indicator terms, a common pattern for the technical manager is the Intuitive Thinker (NT) type, known as the Visionary Leader. Keirsey and Bates identify certain characteristics commonly associated with technical professionals as managers:

> The NT manager is apt to be intellectually oriented and may unknowingly communicate an attitude on his part that he does not value subordinates (or superiors) who are not intellectually gifted. He may find difficulty in his interpersonal transactions because of his projections onto others that they [also] should be thoroughly competent, adequate, and achieving in all possible respects (1984, 146).

A good strategy to improve your relationships and productivity is to work at identifying the positive characteristics of others and focusing on them. It may well be true that someone doesn't possess the same gifts or intellectual abilities that you do, but it's often true that they possess others that also have value and merit. Recognize those characteristics in others, and you will find that they are more likely to recognize your own positive characteristics in return.

22. Is primarily a specialist, not a generalist. Most technical professionals begin their career and put their energies into a specialization, if for no other reason than it's hard to be equally expert in everything. Leadership and management, however, are essentially generalist occupations. In the federal government, your application for the senior executive service— the top level of career (nonpolitical) executives in civil service agencies—must show that you have mastered an executive perspective. One core element is *strategic vision*: "the ability to ensure that key national and organizational goals, priorities, values, and other issues are considered in making program decisions and exercising leadership to implement and to ensure that the organization's mission and strategic vision are reflected in the management of its people" (Troutman et al. 1995, 104).

In other words, an executive reaches past the limits of his previous role, occupation, and specialty in order to embrace the wider vision and values of the organization and its customers.

23. Has unusual hobbies or interests that are pursued with great passion. Whatever the classic technical professional is interested in, she is interested in strongly, often developing in-depth knowledge and knowing all the minutiae of the field. This is actually quite a positive element, unless it goes too far. In one of the trials during the Kenneth Starr investigation of the Clinton Whitewater case, one juror wore her *Star Trek* uniform to the trial. This is an example of someone who will likely not be considered for a senior executive role in the organization, although her job skills may well be excellent. Watch for the danger of boring others with your passions, or acting out those passions in inappropriate environments.

24. Believes authority and respect must be earned by those in power, not automatically assumed. Does this describe you?

> The fact that a certain person proclaims something, whatever his or her title, reputation, or credentials, leaves the NT [Intuitive Thinker] indifferent. The pronouncement must stand on its own merits, tried in the court of coherence, verification, and pragmatics. "I understand that Einstein said so," comments the NT, "but even the best of us can err" (Keirsey and Bates 1984, 49).

It's not necessary or even smart to abandon your own judgment in the face of opposition or a different management direction, but it is necessary to avoid making unnecessary enemies in the process. Authority, like the Law of Gravity, is frequently a fact; whether you believe it to be earned or unearned doesn't change its reality. Recognize the facts and how they affect your ability to do your job. Avoid showing unnecessary negativity toward authority figures.

25. *Feels socially awkward, an outsider.* The introversion that is a classic element of the technical professional may lead to a sense of social awkwardness. Fortunately, like many areas of life, social skills are learned behavior. If you don't have a natural and instinctive liking for social interaction, you may never become great, but you can become competent by choosing to do the work. Business expert Peter Drucker, who coined the term "knowledge worker," points out that such people's productivity depends on their efforts being coordinated as part of an organizational team. Writers are not publishers; computer programmers are not software distributors. In knowledge work, Drucker says, "Teams become the work unit rather than the individual himself"(Goleman 1995, 159–60). It's critical to your productivity, success, and advancement that you develop basic competency in this core area, not only for your leadership role, but also frankly for basic survival in the modern organization.

Exercise 2

Starting Your Personal Action Plan

Based on your answers to the first survey and your reading of the descriptive information, write what you consider to be your three most important challenge areas or weaknesses in succeeding in a leadership role, along with your first thoughts of things you might do to improve those areas.

1. First challenge area

   _____
   _____

   What I could do to improve myself in this area.

   _____
   _____
   _____
   _____
   _____
   _____
   _____

2. Second challenge area

   _____
   _____

What I could do to improve myself in this area.

_____

_____

_____

_____

_____

_____

_____

3. Third challenge area

_____

_____

What I could do to improve myself in this area.

_____

_____

_____

_____

_____

_____

_____

Debrief of Exercise 2

As you continue with this book, look for specific ideas and strategies that relate to the three main areas that you have identified. When you find one, turn back to this section, and add it to your list (using extra paper as necessary). At the end of the book, you'll use this information to create your personal action plan.

Why only three areas? Perhaps you feel that you have more. One important strategy for successful personal change is not to do too much at once. You are better off picking three challenges and working on those, rather than picking twenty-five challenges and working on them all simultaneously. And, of course, nothing stops you from coming back to work on new ones as you have mastered your current set of challenges.

Notes

1. The value of what else you could have done with the resources that you spent on a particular project is known as the *opportunity cost*, for the opportunity you lost by going in the direction that you did.
2. For a chilling example, see: Godwin, Tom, 1970, The Cold Equations, in Silverberg, Robert, ed., *The Science Fiction Hall of Fame: Volume 1*, New York: Doubleday, 447–69.

Chapter 3
Payoffs and Prices

How Technical Professionals View Management

Management as an occupation is not always well thought of by technical professionals. Scott Adams, focusing on office life in a technology organization, developed The Dilbert Principle: "The most ineffective workers are systematically moved to the place where they can do the least damage: management" (1996, 14).

Hardly a ringing recommendation—right? Worse, the same thought may have occurred to you from time to time: "If I were in charge, I'd avoid these obvious mistakes and do it better." Now you're in "put-up-or-shut-up" mode. The problem is often you find that you don't really have the authority that you assumed a manager possessed, and the problems are more intractable than you thought—and the new members of your team are much less enthusiastic about your leadership than you hoped.

Maybe you've already found yourself branded as *the enemy*. People come to you and say, "Ever since you became a manager, you've changed. We thought you understood our problems and would stand up for us, but we still have our problems. You're on their side now."

Where You Stand Depends on Where You Sit

In fact, your point of view *has* changed. Perhaps your team members aren't working as hard as they should. They certainly don't understand the pressure that you're under. They don't seem to have the welfare of the organization and its customers clearly in mind. And maybe they aren't quite as competent and as able as they seem to think they are.

With luck, your situation may not seem as bleak as this. At least, you may only feel this way on odd-numbered days. As a new manager, expect to have good days and bad, times you feel that it will all be successful, and times you wonder why on earth you accepted these new responsibilities and all the hassle that comes with it. (Hint: It probably wasn't for the *big bucks*.)

You have experienced and probably will continue to experience a sense of disruption and change. No matter how successful your transition, it will likely not be smooth or without stress. To reduce the stress, use a combination of self-assessment and self-development.

Exercise 3

Making the Transition Decision

Whether you've already been a manager for some time or whether you're just in the process of making the change, there are losses as well as gains to consider. You may want to complete this self-assessment in multiple sessions, adding new items to your list as you think of them.

What did you love best about your job as a technical professional?

_____

_____

_____

_____

_____

_____

_____

_____

_____

_____

_____

_____

_____

_____

_____

_____

_____

Debrief of Exercise 3

Common positive answers to this question include:
- I got to solve problems and get measurable results.
- I could work independently on my own projects.
- I enjoyed the subject matter of the work itself.
- I liked the feeling of accomplishment and job satisfaction.
- My job was definable and limited.
- It's what I was trained to do.

Common negative answers to this question include:
- I didn't have to go to as many meetings.
- I didn't have to put up with too much office politics or management [censored].
- I got to go home at 5 P.M. most of the time.
- I could leave my job at the office without worrying all the time.

The job of a technical professional tends to be measurable and specific. You get a certain number of projects, which you are to accomplish individually or in a team. While there may be technical challenges or organizational restrictions that make the work difficult, the final result of the work is a specific accomplishment.

There are limits to your need to be involved in the organizational issues, as opposed to your project. You can safely ignore many things that don't directly apply to you.

You can see that there are many attractive qualities about being a technical professional and not worrying about the move into management or a higher rank. You can also see that there is no way that you can continue to keep all these attractive elements while making the transition to a new role as a manager. A sense of loss and frustration, therefore, is inevitable.

People do not tend to do well what they dislike and despise. For you to become successful as a manager, you must accept that there will be a sense of loss in leaving a previous role, but ultimately you must find a sense of payoff and positive personal gain from becoming a manager that outweighs the loss.

Exercise 4

Making the Transition Decision (Continued)

Consider the potential gains in your new situation, using the same format as in the previous exercise. You may want to complete this self-assessment in multiple sessions, adding new items to your list as you think of them. The more different items on your list, the more useful you'll find this exercise.

What are your payoffs for going into management?

Debrief of Exercise 4

Common positive answers to this question include:
- Making more money
- Having more influence and power over people
- Having more control over work situations
- Being included more in the process
- Improving long-term career opportunities
- Expanding and improving professional skills.

Common negative answers to this question include:
- Don't feel like so much like a mushroom (1)
- Don't have to do boring repetitive tasks
- No challenge in the old job
- Avoid excessive overtime
- Less travel.

Gains as well as losses can be both positive and negative, and it's valuable for you to focus on both in making the personal payoff decision for becoming a manager.

You'll find that the more items on your positive list, the easier it will be to make the transition, which is part of the reason you should complete these exercises in multiple sessions over several days.

You can get additional benefit from this exercise by turning your list into a reinforcement tool. Here's how:
1. The first thing each morning, read your list of benefits and payoffs for being a manager.
2. Add one item to the list.

Making this a daily habit is a good way to focus your mental energy on the positives of your situation. When, inevitably, problems and lousy days occur, you'll approach them from a different, and more successful, perspective.

Sound like a *positive thinking* approach? It is. Current biomedical research strongly suggests that optimism is an important predictor of success and achievement. Psychologist Martin Seligman says:

> Literally hundreds of studies show that pessimists give up more easily and get depressed more often. These experiments also show that optimists do much better in school and college, at work and on the playing field. They regularly exceed the predictions of aptitude tests. When optimists run for office, they are more apt to be elected than pessimists are. Their health is unusually good. They age well, much freer than most of us from the usual physical ills of middle age. Evidence suggests they may even live longer (1991, 5).

Your mental attitude about yourself and your new role is an important—a critical—predictor of your ultimate success in a leadership role. If pessimism and negativity are part of your normal style, Dr. Seligman's evidence is that change is possible: "Pessimism is escapable. Pessimists can in fact learn to be optimists, and not through mindless devices like whistling a happy tune or mouthing platitudes … but by learning a new set of cognitive skills" (1991, 5).

The purpose of this exercise is to increase your personal focus on the success factors in your position on a regular and daily basis. Make sure that your answers are yours: it doesn't help to focus on payoffs that you *should* care about or that *everyone else* cares about. Coping with the emotional stress of supervision and management normally requires active self-management on your part.

Don't worry. There is a strong skill set that you have to master to become an effective manager, and many of those skills fit into paradigms with which you are already familiar as a technical professional. You may also be quite familiar with the emotional challenges and issues, but because even the most knowledgeable person in this area has room to improve and grow, it's important that you begin your transition by first focusing on the fundamentals.

It is possible that when you honestly add the payoffs and compare them to the price you have to pay, you may decide that this is not the direction for you. If that's your answer, have the courage of your convictions and get out of management altogether. As management expert Rosina Harter says, "Pain is inevitable. Misery is optional."

The next step in your self-assessment is to use the information you've already discovered to develop a personal action plan.

Exercise 5

Action Steps to Increase Payoffs

If you listed some of the following payoffs for moving into a management or leadership role, circle them and study the action steps recommended. You'll be able to add additional ones at the end of the exercise (Dobson and Dobson 1997, 32–37).

YES   NO   Making more money.

If this is one of your payoffs for going into management, you may be disappointed, at least at the first-level rank. Initially, managers get a little more pay for a lot more responsibility. At higher levels, the financial payoff is likely to be greater. If the money is your main goal, is this the best route to get it? What steps can you take to improve your financial rewards?

Possible Action Steps:
1. Find out about bonus or merit-pay opportunities.
2. Negotiate for a raise, either now or after achieving a certain objective.
3. Determine what others with similar responsibilities are making, both inside and outside your organization.
4. Understand the financial situation of your organization.
5. Get training and developmental assignments to increase your skills ... and your worth.
6. Figure what you're worth on the open market.

Add your own steps:
7. _____
8. _____
9. _____

YES   NO   Having more influence and power over people.

Nice people aren't supposed to seek power over others. The reality is that the exercise of power can be enjoyable and rewarding. Nor is there anything wrong with this, as long as the power isn't used in destructive or harmful ways. Power and authority can be used in constructive ways. You can focus attention on key problems and issues, motivate people to achieve more, and help others in their personal and professional growth. You may be frustrated that people don't seem to respect your supervisory authority, don't do what you need them to do, or don't value your attempts to help them. Remember that influence and power over others requires their consent. Ultimately, you must develop a relationship of mutual consensual development with your employees. What steps can you take to develop your leadership skills, or to earn respect and obedience from others, or to influence people toward your goals?

Possible Action Steps:
1. Get training in leadership/motivational skills.
2. Get feedback from team members about your leadership effectiveness.
3. Get feedback from your management about your leadership effectiveness.
4. Apply the new techniques that you learn, giving them time to work.
5. Negotiate common goals that motivate others to do what you want.

Add your own steps:
6. _____
7. _____
8. _____

YES   NO   Having more control over work situations.

A powerful reason for seeking management authority is to have more control over work situations. You may have been frustrated at the direction of your department or of the corporate mission. You may feel that management has not been doing the right thing. Now you're in a position of authority and control. You try to use your position to make changes and achieve control. Instead, you find yourself being fought in all directions—staff and management. The status quo has substantial inertia, and change always is harder and slower than you expect. What could you do to increase your legitimate control?

Possible Action Steps:
1. Volunteer for committee/task force assignments that might increase your influence.
2. List the changes that you think should be made, rank them by order of desirability/difficulty, and start by working toward one single change.
3. Read management books on the topics of your concern, and look for strategies that might help. (See the Bibliography at the end of this book for ideas.)
4. Build relationships with key managers to increase your influence.
5. Make sure that your basic job is under control before pushing for major changes.

Add your own steps:
6. _____
7. _____
8. _____

YES   NO   Being included more in the process.

A high need for inclusion motivates many people to seek management responsibilities. Most people want to be part of the process, to be asked, to be part of the decisions, to be part of the group that counts. Yet it seems that every time you turn around, you discover meetings to which you weren't invited, decisions made seemingly behind your back, and people who seem to want to *include you out*. What steps can you take to increase your inclusion?

Possible Action Steps:
1. Study networking techniques, and develop a plan to build better relationships.
2. Ask others about their duties, responsibilities, and goals, and ask how you can help them.
3. Get feedback from trusted associates about how your personality affects your ability to be included.
4. Volunteer for committees and special project team assignments.
5. Join trade and industry associations to increase your range of contacts.

Add your own steps:
6. _____
7. _____
8. _____

YES   NO   Improving my long-term career opportunities.

Even if your immediate financial rewards are not very great, the long-term potential on the management track is often substantial. Unfortunately, you may find yourself so deeply immersed in unsolvable problems and no-win situations that you sometimes wonder if you were set to fail. It's important to remember that you cannot delegate responsibility for your career growth; you must plan and act. Advancement doesn't come via the *talent fairy*; it only comes through your own efforts. What can you do to increase your long-term career opportunities?

Possible Action Steps:
1. Seek training opportunities both inside and outside the organization.
2. Consider enrolling in after-hours or weekend graduate studies on your own initiative.
3. Ask for developmental assignments to increase your long-term worth to the organization.
4. Get feedback on your strengths and weaknesses, and develop plans for personal and professional improvement.
5. Get involved in trade and industry organizations.

Add your own steps:
6. _____
7. _____
8. _____

YES   NO   Expanding and improving my professional skills.

Not only are you likely motivated by money and career growth, but most people are also motivated by the opportunity to develop new skills. Unfortunately, you often find yourself stuck having to do the same things over and over again, usually because you're the most experienced and technically capable member of your own team. (That's often a reason why you are where you are today.) What can you do to improve and expand your professional skills?

Possible Action Steps:
1. Work on your delegation skills to help your team grow by delegating to it more of your previous responsibilities.
2. Look for training and development opportunities.
3. Seek new work assignments that stretch you in new directions.
4. Remind your managers about your range of skills so that you'll get opportunities in new areas.
5. Identify some specific skills that you want to develop, and create an action plan to learn and practice them on the job.
6. Make sure that you aren't getting stuck in perfectionism: let others do their jobs *good enough*, even if you could do them better.

Add your own steps:
7. _____
8. _____
9. _____

Additional payoffs. The more individual payoffs you can list, the more energy you can focus on becoming a more effective supervisor.

Additional payoffs for supervising:
_____
_____
_____
_____
_____

Possible action steps for each payoff:
1. _____
2. _____
3. _____
4. _____
5. _____
6. _____
7. _____
8. _____
9. _____
10. _____

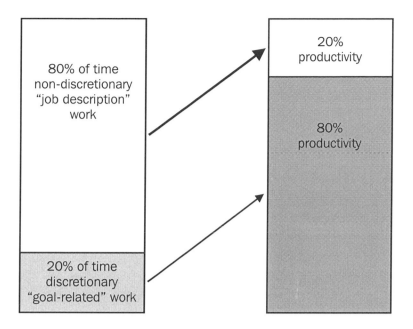

Figure 2   The Pareto Principle

Debrief of Exercise 5

"Life," the saying goes, "is what happens to you when you're making other plans." Your professional career consists of *job-description* priorities and goal-related activities. They are subject to the Pareto Principle, generally known as the *80/20 rule*: 80 percent of your work gives you 20 percent of your results, and 20 percent of your work gives you 80 percent of your results (2).

You don't have a lot of choice in performing the job-description work, but you need to focus on maximizing the payoff from the approximately 20 percent of the time available for your high-payoff, results-oriented, goal-related priorities.

Take some of the action steps that you've identified in the previous exercise, and start by inserting them into your regular *to-do* list or time management/priority management system (Temme 1993, 16–17).

Notes

1. "I must be a mushroom. People keep me in the dark, they feed me manure, and then they can me" (Office Cartoon).
2. Vilfredo Pareto (1848–1923), an Italian economist and political philosopher, analyzed the distribution of wealth in Italy. He discovered that most of it was in the hands of a few people (the vital few), while the majority (the trivial many) existed in poverty. Peter Drucker in *Managing for Results* suggested that many management problems follow this principle. You also will likely encounter the Pareto chart, one of the basic tools of total quality management, which involves analysis to determine the "vital few" problems separate from the "trivial many." The 80/20 ratio, which was noted by Pareto in his original research, has become a rule of thumb that fits numerous situations.

Chapter 4
Management:
It's Not Just a Job;
It's a Career Change

The Changing Skill Mix

It's ironic and paradoxical that the transition from technical professional to manager works as illustrated in the sidebar, *How to Become a Manager*.

Moving from technical professional to manager isn't a promotion; it's a career change. The elements of success change, the goals change, and the methodology changes. The ratio of what you do on a day-to-day basis changes. As you continue the path of your advancement, you will find that a constantly changing skill mix is necessary. Focus your efforts on what you need for the next job rather than on what you need to succeed in yesterday's job.

Making the Transition

from Technical Professional	→	to a Leadership Role
Orientation around things/ideas	→	Orientation around people
Concern for self	→	Concern for others
Focus on short term	→	Focus on long term
Problems clearly defined	→	Problems *fuzzy*
Many problems solvable	→	Most problems only *manageable*

Things/ideas to people. Technical work tends by its nature to involve things and ideas at its core. Even in a profession such as medicine, if one is not careful, the focus tends to be on the illness rather than on the person. In a recent novel, a judge is talking about being treated for breast cancer. "What I'm gladdest of—proud of—is that I didn't become the disease. You know that starts in the hospital. They act as if you don't have a name. They identify you by the procedure. 'You're a mastectomy'" (Turow 1996, 209). While this attitude can be—and often is—considered callous, there are two important reasons why it is common: 1) the technical professionals are there for the work, and so concentrate on the work itself, and 2) there is a need for emotional protection for the practitioners under difficult circumstances.

How to Become a Manager

1. Management thinks that you're doing a good job.
2. Therefore, it tells you to stop doing it.
3. Instead, it wants you to do a new and different job.
4. It's a job for which you probably haven't been trained.
5. It's a job that involves different strengths and abilities, by and large, from the ones that have made you successful up to now.
6. Management doesn't know with certainty whether you have the ability, temperament, or skills to be successful at it.
7. Congratulations! You're a manager!

The management side is all about people. As organizational development expert Rosina Harter observed, "Your job is no longer to assemble the widgets, nor even to make sure the widgets are assembled. Your job is to get the people to assemble the widgets."

Self to others. One great advantage of being a technical professional is that your success and your failure can be laid at your own doorstep. As a manager, your success and your failure are subject to the performance of your team. Many managers come to the ironic realization that if your choice were to be personally competent with a poor staff, or personally incompetent with a brilliant and productive staff, then the second choice would lead to better results. Caring for your staff, providing effective staff development, supporting your staff, and helping your staff to succeed are the strategies that help you achieve your goals.

Short term to long term. Regardless of the time horizon of your projects, the management time horizon is always longer. Pushing your perspective past the short term, the immediate, into the long term is one of your challenges. What's different about the long term? First, there's achieving the company mission and vision. If you have one of those mission statements that includes words like, "Our mission is to provide world-class quality and unparalleled customer service as the leading producer in our market, while valuing the diversity of our work force members as key contributors to stakeholder value," then you may have thought that this was just hot air. And maybe it was—depending on the extent of real management commitment that existed.

On the other hand, such a goal can be real and legitimate as long as it's understood that the time horizon can be years or even decades. You may not have "world-class quality" today; you may not be able to achieve it in the next year to two years, but you can achieve it over time.

Problem solving may also be long term. James H. Austin tells this story:

> One day a doctor had a vision of a long line of patients waiting to see him—a line extending far out of his office and into the street. He already knew what the diagnosis was: each patient had a sprained ankle from stepping into the deep hole in the

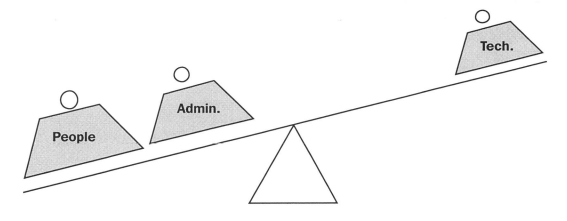

Figure 3   Balancing Technical and Management Skills

sidewalk out in front of the office. The doctor knew the source of his own dilemma. He was just too busy seeing patients in pain with sprained ankles. He never could take the time to go out and repair the sidewalk (from Austin's *Chase, Chance and Creativity*, quoted in Temme 1993, 22).

The *value added* of management is making sure that you fix the sidewalk.

Problems clearly defined to problems fuzzy. If there is a right answer, then the problem is almost by definition a minor problem. Minor problems should be delegated to your team members. Major problems are defined by the following characteristics:

- Key facts are unknown and unknowable.
- Outcomes are difficult to predict.
- Multiple variables, many not subject to control, affect the outcome.
- Major organizational issues and/or lots of money are at stake.
- Precedents are not clearly applicable or even available.
- Numerous people have interests not only in the successful outcome but also in the methods used to get there.
- A *right* answer may not even exist.

You know you're a real manager when you discover that you're not being paid to make good decisions as much as you are to make decisions when all alternatives are risky and unpleasant.

Problems solvable to problems manageable. Another definition of an *easy* problem is one that has an answer at all. Many management problems aren't solvable, in the common sense of the term. Instead, the problems may be *manageable*, meaning that your job is to cope with them and minimize their interference while accepting the reality that they won't go away.

An example of a manageable problem is coping with too few staff to handle an expanding workload. The obvious solution (more staff) is not possible in your organizational reality. You cannot *solve* the problem. Instead, you look for ways to minimize the problem, streamline the work, and get around it the best that you can.

Managers receive more money than do nonmanagers, not because their jobs are necessarily more difficult, but because they are rather more risky. Despite the *fuzziness* and uncertainty associated with management decisions, you, the manager, are still held personally responsible—like the captain of a ship. Even if your lieutenant was at the helm and you were

---

The Godzilla Principle

In Japanese monster movies, there's frequently a scene where the Japanese movie monster *du jour* (Godzilla, Mothra, Gamora, and so on) is a little, baby, cute monster. People say, "Oh, what a cute little monster!" Obviously, there is no urgency. They ignore the monster.

They wait until the monster is full grown and busily stomping downtown Tokyo; then you hear them shout, "What are we going to do?"

The answer is, of course, little or nothing. When Godzilla is rampaging through downtown Tokyo, there's very little you can do about it. The best options are all now in the past.

In your work, spend time in *baby-monster patrol*. Every time you find a little problem with the power to grow into a big one later, stomp on it at once. That's the Godzilla Principle: The earlier you catch a problem, the easier it is to solve.

Source: Dobson 1996, 12–13

---

asleep when the ship ran aground, you are still responsible. Accepting and coping with that responsibility is one of the most difficult challenges of leadership. You can in fact be fired from your position because of a problem that you didn't create and a solution that you didn't design or implement—just because you happened to be there.

Management Surprises

Certain aspects of this discussion are areas with which you were already familiar, and others may be new to you. This leads us to the area of *management surprises*.

Effective planners and project managers always evaluate projects after they are completed with the goal of extracting lessons for the future.

One interesting variation of this technique is to focus on surprises rather than on problems. If you anticipated that a problem might occur, and it did occur, then you have the value of your anticipation and planning that you did in advance to minimize the effect of the Godzilla Principle.

On the other hand, if you didn't know a problem might occur, and it did, then you are surprised. Godzilla has snuck into Tokyo the back way. Obviously, if you didn't expect the problem, you didn't plan for it, and you're in worse shape as a result. (This is true whether or not you could have been expected to anticipate it—an example of the inexorable Law of Gravity situation again.)

In the evaluation process, the best strategy for maximizing future performance is to focus on surprises—good surprises as well as unpleasant ones—and figure how you could anticipate a surprise next time, and how such foreknowledge could improve your ability to handle it.

Case Study 3

You Knew That the Job Was Dangerous When You Took It

"I can't believe they blamed it on me!" Thomas cried.

In fact, the situation was pretty ambiguous. Thomas had been given responsibility for promoting the distribution tickets for a series of special presentations on the company's new product. Ads encouraged people to call, and the department secretary—who didn't report to Thomas—fielded calls and took reservations.

Because of a communications mix-up, the secretary gave each caller reserved tickets to all of the events in the series. By the time the second event was promoted, all the tickets were gone!

Thomas' argument was: 1) the secretary didn't report to me, 2) no one told me that I was responsible for communicating the information to the secretary, 3) I did communicate it, and 4) I was responsible only for promoting the distribution, not managing it.

Certainly there's a good argument for Thomas' position, but the reality is that managers are held responsible. Even though lines of authority were unclear, Thomas needed to take the initiative and do the follow-up because no one else had the responsibility. If Thomas weren't in management, however, then he probably wouldn't have been blamed.

Exercise 6

Surprise, Surprise, Surprise!

In this exercise, focus on surprises in your new role as a manager or leader.

What about the transition to management has been most surprising to you?

_____
_____
_____
_____
_____
_____

What didn't you expect?

_____
_____
_____
_____
_____
_____
_____

What did you expect that didn't happen?

_____
_____
_____
_____
_____
_____
_____

What might you have done differently if you had expected these things?

_____
_____
_____
_____
_____
_____
_____

What can you do differently and better as a result of this exercise?

_____
_____
_____
_____
_____
_____
_____

Debrief of Exercise 6

Focusing on surprises in this manner is a valuable technique, and one that you can use in situations other than this. In addition to the impact of the surprise situation itself, the fact of surprises often adds disproportionately to the stress of management.

How do your answers in this exercise relate to the problems and payoffs that you've uncovered in earlier exercises? How do the action items in Exercise 5 relate to the surprises and action steps that you identified here? How do the personality characteristics that you identified in Exercise 1 relate to the surprises that you encountered? Did they help or hinder, make the surprises more likely or less likely?

Revisit this exercise from time to time, because surprises are unlikely to stop as you move ahead through your supervisory career.

As a manager, you are entrusted with responsibility for certain company assets. Never forget that you are one of those assets, and that you have a responsibility not only to yourself, but also to your organization—to take care of yourself for the long-term good of the organization.

Section Two
THE ART, CRAFT, AND SCIENCE OF MANAGEMENT

The definition of *management* in Chambers Concise 20th Century Dictionary (besides such self-referential definitions as "the art or act of managing") is: "a manner of directing or of using anything." A manager (besides "one who manages") is: "in an industrial firm or business, a person who deals with administration and with the design and marketing, etc., of the product, as opposed to its actual construction" and "one who organizes other peoples' doings."

Associated with the concept of management are also to:

- train by exercise, as a horse
- handle, wield, conduct, administer
- be at the head of
- deal tactfully with
- contrive successfully
- have time for
- be able to cope with
- manipulate
- bring about
- conduct affairs
- get on

as well as:

- skillful treatment
- controlling, administering, domineering.

And all of them are part of your responsibilities and new behaviors in your new role.

In this section, you will explore and refresh yourself with fundamental management concepts, theories, and practices. Because of the *career change* nature of management, it's vital for you to master certain key skills in order to achieve your goals and move ahead.

Chapter 5

The Mission of Management

A Mission Statement for a Manager

As a manager and a supervisor, your mission (1) is to achieve certain work and project goals using a limited assortment of resources, which include staff, budget, and equipment.

To do so, you perform certain actions and use skills that include communication, delegation, recruitment, planning, training, motivation, behavior modification, systems development, conflict management, and problem solving.

You do this within the context of your personal style, a chosen leadership style, and the style of the organization of which you are a part.

You do this with respect to the staff that report to you; to project team members and others over whom you have indirect authority at best; to your own managers and supervisors in the hierarchy of the organization; to other departments in the organization whose cooperation you need; to contractors, suppliers, and others who perform work on your goals; and to customers and outsiders in order to achieve common goals.

You do this given a specific and limited (and usually insufficient) amount of resources and formal authority, and must develop and use political and organizational skills to get the remaining resources and authority necessary to accomplish goals.

And you are held fully accountable for the outcome.

The Real World of Management and Supervision

A common complaint of those who enter management ranks is that they frequently have done the job for quite a while before the title and promotion shows up. Such semi-official positions as *team leader, acting supervisor, project manager*, and *coordinator* often serve as the first rung of management.

A lower-stress way to look at this situation is that you are being auditioned for the role. It's easier and less damaging to remove someone from an *acting* position that was never stated to be permanent than it is to demote someone who was given official rank.

The irony, unfortunately, is that for many people their introduction to supervision is under circumstances of lower-than-usual power and authority; without much age, experience, or rank differential between supervisor and staff; and without much training and support in the new functions. Too many people must learn to supervise and manage, as the saying goes, "the way the cat learned to swim."

Case Study 4

B-O-S-S Spelled Backwards Is Double-S-O-B

"When I first became a supervisor," Jack said, "I was so naive I actually believed that meant people would do what I said!"

Jack was faced with the situation of supervising a team of technical professionals who were skilled at their work, had direct contact with managers and customers throughout the organization, and had their own ideas about the right way to do the work.

His mandate—so he thought—was to take charge of an unruly staff and streamline the process of the work. He quickly discovered that his team members ignored the major initiatives and changes that he proposed, arguing that they already knew the best way and that he didn't have the experience.

Jack used his supervisory authority to order them to obey. That worked for about a week. Then one person, Bruce, went to Jack's boss to complain. Jack's boss listened to Bruce sympathetically and asked him to give Jack a chance, then suggested to Jack that he move a little slower.

But the damage was done. From then on, any initiative Jack tried resulted in visits by his staff to Jack's boss. Quickly, Jack discovered that his supervisory authority meant little or nothing. Nevertheless, Jack's boss continued to put pressure on Jack to improve his operation's efficiency.

Even when your position becomes official, you often discover that the gap between the power that you have and the power that you need is great, and the support still may not be there.

Jack's mistake (see the sidebar)—and an easy trap for new managers to fall into—was moving too quickly and using his formal authority as a primary tool. Experienced supervisors learn that formal authority is generally the last tool to use, not the first. Which is possibly one reason why new supervisors have to perform without much of it.

Exercise 7

First Challenges of Management

1. How would your boss—not you—define your current official role as a manager? Is your official authority in writing, or informal?

_____

_____

_____

_____

_____

2. List the resources (people, tools, systems) that are technically under your authority. Specifically, how much official control do you have over each resource?

_____

_____

_____

_____

_____

3. What authority (if any) do you have to make or approve purchases, negotiate and approve contracts, or make other decisions that bind your organization legally or financially?

_____

_____

_____

_____

_____

4. Do you select your own team members, are they selected for you, or is there a hybrid responsibility?

_____

_____

_____

_____

_____

5. What resources (people, budget, systems, tools) that you regularly use and need don't report to you in an official capacity? How does that affect the level of cooperation you receive?

_____

_____

_____

_____

_____

6. Who is responsible for setting departmental, group, or individual goals for your team? Is it you, you and your supervisor, members of the team themselves, customers, senior management, or some combination? Where do you fit?

_____

_____

_____

_____

_____

7. Do you have direct access to senior management (above your own supervisor), customers, other department heads, and so on, or do you have to go through intervening management (internal or external)? Do your peers and superiors accept you as a technical authority? Do you regularly attend top-level meetings impacting your work?

_____

_____

_____

_____

_____

8. At what point do you have to gain the approval of others higher in the organization to make project-related decisions? Do you have enough respect and acceptance from higher authority for your recommendations to be seriously considered?

_____

_____

_____

_____

_____

Debrief of Exercise 7

The purpose and value of this exercise is to start you thinking about your current official level of responsibility and authority, and to identify any major gaps between what you need and what you've got. Take the time to write fully your answers to each question, using extra paper. It's important to write this; you'll see it more clearly and be able to use it more effectively if it's in black and white.

You may find this exercise somewhat depressing when you realize how little real authority you have. Here's where politics and power come into the equation: the real power to manage your work and your team is not what others give you; it's what you make and what you take. By developing both unofficial and official power within the organization, you can reduce the size and scope of your dilemma and gain improved—though always less than total—control over your situation.

Styles of Supervision and Management

There is more than one route to supervisory effectiveness. To be an effective supervisor and manager, you must select an approach that works for you and fits your situation. This is called a "supervisory style," and a lot of leadership training material focuses on your style choices.

Alphabet Soup

The classic dichotomy of leadership is between the Theory X and Theory Y approaches. Theory X is based on three key assumptions (2):

1. The average person has an inherent dislike of work and will avoid it, if possible.
2. Most people will not work toward objectives unless controlled, directed, and threatened with punishment.
3. The average person prefers to be directed, wants to avoid responsibility, has little ambition, and wants security above all else.

   Theory Y is based on six assumptions about people:
1. Work is as natural as play or rest.
2. External control and threats are not the only way to motivate workers.
3. Commitment to objectives is a motivator.
4. Workers can learn not only to accept but also to seek responsibility.
5. Ingenuity and creativity are widely distributed in the population.
6. Most people's intellectual potential is only partly utilized in the organization.

   More recently, Theory Z (Ouchi 1981) has been advanced as an alternative approach. This approach is an American adaptation of key aspects of Japanese management style, especially in the area of mutual trust building, greater employee involvement and empowerment, and the flexible organization. Such concepts are now widespread, and show up in the works of numerous management authors.

   The reality is that Theory X, Theory Y, and Theory Z all have places and situations in which they have proven effective. Therefore, the concept of style flexibility, or "different strokes for different folks," has come back to the fore. Tony Alessandra, in his audio program, *Mastering Your Message* (1997), refers to the Platinum Rule: "Do unto others as they would like to be done unto."

Which Is Right for You?

The appropriate management and supervisory style depends on a number of variables:

- your own natural personality
- the natural personalities of individual team members (3)
- the level of work experience of each individual team member
- the nature of the work to be performed
- the organizational style and culture
- the level of commitment and drive of the individual team members
- situations that can increase and lower morale, self-confidence, and productivity.

   The two basic styles are *task-centered* (Theory X) and *people-centered* (Theory Y) [Brown and Dudley 1989, 1–4]. Task-centered managers provide clear and definite instructions, define procedures and steps, and make decisions—they tell what, how, and when. People-centered managers listen and discuss suggestions with team members. They trust others and care about them as people.

Combining Styles

It's obvious that neither by itself solves all work-related issues. Ken Blanchard, of *One Minute Manager* fame, created the Situational Leadership II model, which balances the two elements in a useful and applicable manner (Blanchard, Carew, and Parisi-Carew 1990, 68–110).

A manager can exhibit high and low amounts of the two behaviors, which Blanchard calls "directive" (task-centered) and "supportive" (people-centered). A directing style (S1) is high directive and low supportive behavior. It's most appropriate for new team members, who often have enthusiasm and commitment, but little knowledge or skill. A coaching style (S2), high in both elements, is for people who are struggling with the tasks as well as coping with lack of self-confidence. They need both direction and support. A supporting style (S3) is high supportive, but low directive. Team members with high skill levels, but variable self-confidence and morale, need this approach. The final stage, the delegating style (S4), is low in both elements. Peak performers who have both the skill and the self-motivation can do the work with minimal interference.

As a supervisor, your job is to match the appropriate behavior mix (S1, S2, S3, or S4) with the developmental level of the individual or team (called D1, D2, D3, or D4, to match the supervisory styles). Among the advantages of this model is that it helps you as a supervisor adjust to changing situations and to be aware of how your style affects the performance of your team.

According to a research study of the effects of a rigid management style on team members, authoritarian (Theory X) leaders routinely rated their employees' work less favorably than did democratic (Theory Y) leaders. The authoritarian style, according to software engineering expert Watts S. Humphrey, "not only demotivates people, but it also actually damages them" (1997, 234).

Philip's situation (see the sidebar, *Case Study 5*) is difficult, but not that uncommon. It's vital that you find positive characteristics in team members and work to develop them, not only for their benefit, but also for the sake of your own image of them.

Case Study 5

Can't Live With Them, Can't Kill Them

"My basic problem as a manager was that I didn't like and didn't respect my employees," Philip said.

Philip had been promoted to head his technical department because of his previous management experience (gained elsewhere), and the fact that he was a few years older than most of his team members. From the time he'd joined the company, he had made it clear that he thought that the others were simply not as bright or as able as he. He had obviously been persuasive enough to get the leadership role.

The problem, of course, is that his attitude made it very difficult to select and use a supervisory style that worked. It's hard to camouflage a negative opinion; it tends to express itself. Philip did choose an appropriate mix of task- and people-centeredness, but he found that he couldn't implement it effectively, because others saw as patronizing—if not downright dishonest—any supportive behaviors that he exhibited.

Every initiative was greeted with resistance; every change that he tried to make was seen as an attempt to get rid of people. The resistance to his authority provoked him and made him want to clamp down harder, which started a feedback cycle that only made it worse.

"The worst thing about that job is that I could see what was happening, including my own contributions, and I still couldn't do anything about it," Philip observed.

In less than a year, he was removed from the supervisory role and given a lateral assignment with no staff. Three months later he left the organization.

Exercise 8

Looking on the Bright Side

For yourself, your supervisor, and each of your team members, select at least five words from the following list that honestly apply to that person.

Active	Deliberate	Gracious	Open-minded
Ambitious	Determined	Helpful	Poised
Animated	Discerning	Honest	Prepared
Assertive	Efficient	Humble	Progressive
Capable	Energetic	Imaginative	Punctual
Communicates well	Enthusiastic	Individualist	Reliable
Competent	Exciting	Industrious	Sincere
Complete	Fair	Insightful	Strong leader
Concise	Faithful	Inspiring	Technically sophisticated
Confident	Forceful	Intelligent	Temperate
Considerate	Friendly	Interested in others	Trustworthy
Consistent	Genuine	Loyal	Truthful
Courageous	Good grammar	Moderate	Versatile
Courteous	Good listener	Modest	Visionary
Creative	Good organizer	Natural	Well-informed
Dedicated	Good problem solver	Observant	Well-read

YOU _____   YOUR SUPERVISOR _____

_____   _____
_____   _____
_____   _____
_____   _____
_____   _____

TEAM MEMBER _____   TEAM MEMBER _____

_____   _____
_____   _____
_____   _____
_____   _____

TEAM MEMBER _____   TEAM MEMBER _____

_____   _____
_____   _____
_____   _____
_____   _____

TEAM MEMBER _____ TEAM MEMBER _____

_____ _____
_____ _____
_____ _____
_____ _____

Debrief of Exercise 8

"Most of us are such conformists," observed Oscar Wilde, "that in the presence of genius, we too would show talent." One of the most documented psychological phenomena is how our attitudes about others affect their behavior and performance. If you think that you have a staff of malcontent incompetents, then you probably do, and if you think that you have a staff of top-flight creative professionals, then you probably do as well—even if they are exactly the same people! By thinking better of others, you change their performance.

Using the positive characteristics lists that you have developed, set as a goal that you will identify and verbally recognize positive behaviors, talents, and skills in others on a daily basis. Not only does positive reinforcement change their behaviors, but it also changes your opinion, which also reinforces their behavioral change (4).

Choosing Your Supervisory Style

What Tom Peters and Robert Waterman say about corporate chief executives also applies to supervisors and team leaders: "It appears that the real role of the chief executive is to manage the values of the organization" (1982, 26).

Use the next exercise to help you choose an appropriate supervisory style to fit your situation.

Exercise 9

Choosing an Appropriate Supervisory Style

Circle the situations that apply to your current work environment to see the overall emphasis that you should put on task-centered versus people-centered behaviors in your supervisory style.

High Task	High People	High Both	Low Both
Complex technology, inexperienced employees	Volunteers or employees who don't formally report to you but who know the work	Stressful environment, high uncertainty	Self-sufficient, capable workers performing complex job
Simple, repetitive tasks that must be done correctly	Very talented "prima donnas"	Employees dislike the work	Peak performers on independent projects
Inexperienced but well-meaning employees	New project or startup, vague job descriptions	Emotionally immature workers, average skill level	R&D and development work with top team but ill-defined goals
New employees	Experienced employees with variable morale	Employees gaining experience	Self-motivated peak performers
Total	Total	Total	Total

Debrief of Exercise 9

As you total the answers in different columns, notice that in most circumstances you must apply more than one supervisory style in your position. You'll also discover that if you revisit this exercise from time to time, your style issues will change.

While the Situational Leadership II model's goal is for employees and teams to move from the lower development levels to the higher (D1 to D4), with the supervisor's style adapting and growing with the team members, this is not always the only or exclusive goal to pursue. Based on the nature of the work and the organizational culture, certain situations may be limited in terms of style growth.

What you should do is make sure that your style flexibility across the spectrum is great, your ability to use both people-centered and task-centered management techniques is developed, and your willingness to adapt to your team in order to help its members grow are all core characteristics of your supervisory style.

Notes

1. "should you decide to accept it"—don't forget that's really an option.
2. For a good discussion of these styles, see Carr-Ruffino 1993, 298–327.
3. For information on personality styles and type indicators, see Dobson 1999a.
4. For more specific tools and techniques in this area, see Dobson and Dobson 2000, 80–85 and elsewhere.

Chapter 6
Communications and Leadership

Situation and Direction

Getting control of your situation and picking your direction is the first great challenge of leadership and supervision. Understanding and applying the daily skills of management is the next level.

You've seen that effective leadership and management is a complex and multifaceted process, as complicated and elegant in its way as any technical project. Unlike normal technical work, however, it is fraught with uncertainty and psychological complexity.

The McKinsey 7-S Framework, which Tom Peters uses as one of the basic tools in *In Search of Excellence*, is intended as a model for organizational development and evaluation. However, it also provides a good framework for the actions and opportunities for influence given to a manager.

This model is one of interrelationships: each element acts and reacts with all the others.

Structure: Describes the formal organization of your team. Is it hierarchical, matrix, or team oriented? How is the work organized? What formal tools or processes are used to control and oversee the work?

Systems: Includes evaluation tools, reporting mechanisms, project management, quality assurance, and other ways to manage the work.

Style: The supervisory style issues that you studied in the previous chapter are critical influencers.

Staff: Not only hiring and firing, but also training and development, career planning, morale and motivation, team building, communications, and conflict resolution.

Skills: Supervisory and leadership skills for yourself; both technical and people skills for your team members. Consider using individual development plans for each team member to focus on important growth issues and how to acquire the necessary skills.

Strategy: Organizational strategy, project strategy, departmental strategy, and team strategy. How will you get where you're going?

Shared Values: At the center of the model, the concept of how we choose to work together for a common goal. Your concerns are twofold: developing/helping to develop the values and the communication and negotiation to ensure that they are truly shared.

Of course, you have to adapt your strategies in these areas to fit within the overall corporate culture of the organization and the nature of the work. Keep your focus on how these elements work together to achieve your goals.

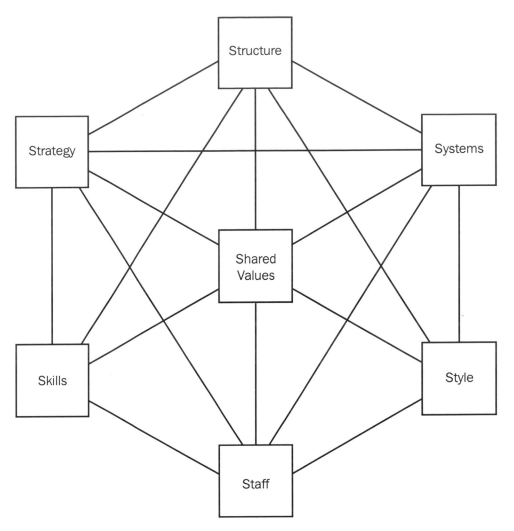

Source: Peters and Waterman Jr. 1982, 9

Figure 4   The McKinsey 7-S Framework

Communications

"What we have here," as the chain gang leader said to Cool Hand Luke, "is a failure to communicate."

"If you don't ask," the saying goes, "you don't get." That's true even when people are willing to help you, on the grounds that if you don't tell people what you want, it's not a good idea to assume that they can read your mind.

Virtually every aspect of the McKinsey 7-S Framework and any other management model that you care to use is built on an assumption of good communication, especially on the part of managers. This is often a shaky assumption. Management expert Peter Drucker once attributed 60 percent of organizational problems to poor or ineffective communication. Of all the reasons to get into trouble in a management or leadership role, poor communications is both the most common and the most easily avoided.

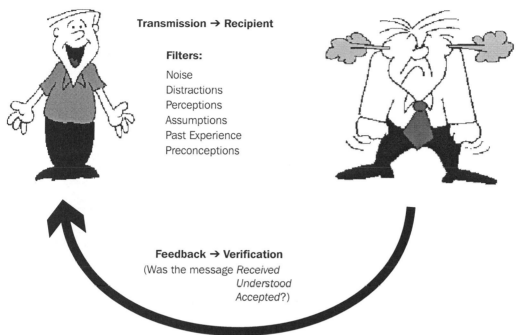

Language → Thought
(interprets semantic content and emotional content)

Transmission → Recipient

Filters:
Noise
Distractions
Perceptions
Assumptions
Past Experience
Preconceptions

Feedback → Verification
(Was the message *Received*
Understood
Accepted?)

Figure 5   The Transmission Model of Communication

To understand why poor communication is so common, and to develop a strategy to avoid such problems, consider the following model for effective communication.

Stage 1: From Thought to Language

Any communication we make originates as a thought, but in the absence of telepathic ability, we must code our thought into language. Not only is this the first of many opportunities for error in the transmission process (we may select the wrong codes), but there also are other problems.

Connotation and denotation. Words and phrases possess both denotation (what they literally mean) and connotation (the associations that they evoke). Connotative meanings can be unintentional (the experience of offending someone with a word or phrase that you didn't intend to have negative meanings) or self-revelatory (betraying feelings and attitudes that you would rather have kept hidden, such as dislike, distrust, or concerns about the ability of a team member to do the work). The controversy over words and phrases known as *political correctness* (*developmentally challenged* versus *handicapped* or *retarded*) is an argument over connotation. (The term *politically correct* itself is an example of putting a negative connotation on words whose denotative meanings are at least neutral, if not positive—after all, *correct* is generally considered a good thing [1].)

Grammar and usage. There are two types of grammar errors: those that only experts notice, and those that everyone notices. Most people have had the embarrassing experience of making a grammatical error around someone who knew better, only to get a patronizing

---

Case Study 6

"Paranoia Strikes Deep (into Your Heart It Will Creep)"

Julie was incensed when she read her email. Her boss had assigned her to manage a complex technical project with another division. The division had sent through a long email addressed to her boss, with a c.c. (courtesy copy) to her. All well and good—the initial contact was through the boss.

Her boss replied to the email. Again, all well and good—but instead of c.c.'ing her, he b.c.c.'d (blind courtesy copied) her. That means that the other division didn't know that she was still in the loop.

"This undercuts my authority and credibility," she fumed. "They'll think this is all meant to be run through my boss."

She sent her boss an email. "Why didn't you copy me directly on the email?" she asked. "What were you trying to accomplish by making me look out of the loop?"

Although the situation was resolved satisfactorily, Julie ended up having a long, emotionally charged meeting with her boss. Why was she b.c.c.'d? It turned out that it was just a mistake—no conscious thought in it.

The denotative elements of Julie's email were clear. However, the connotation—the hidden message—was, "You are trying to undercut or sabotage me," and that message came through to the boss loud and clear, as did the strength of Julie's anger.

Anger is not necessarily inappropriate as a management response, and sometimes getting angry with a boss is the best way to resolve certain situations. However, follow these rules:

1. Get angry in person (and privately), never in writing or by email.
2. Never attribute to malice what can satisfactorily be explained by stupidity or carelessness.
3. Be goal oriented in your anger: decide what behavioral changes you want and focus on those, not on expressing your emotions.
4. Only show your anger on issues that are really important, and don't make it a habit.
5. Rehearse your anger and give yourself some cool-down time before you respond.

---

look and the feeling that the other person has just deducted twenty points from your IQ. (Perhaps you've done this to others.) Among the many reasons to ensure that your grammar and usage are of professional business quality is the effect that it has on the perceptions of other people. An otherwise well-delivered message can be undercut by incorrect grammar and usage; the respect that others have for you may also be affected. The same concerns apply to vocabulary. (You might also watch for a common problem among technical professionals: the use of words that you've read but never heard spoken. Obviously, you're likely to mispronounce them, so that it may be a good idea to check your dictionary regularly, especially if your vocabulary tends to be obfuscatory, prolix, and sesquipedalian (2)—something on which certain technical professionals pride themselves. Don't forget that if your audience doesn't understand your message, your communication has failed.)

Emotional content. Every communication has two kinds of meaning: actual semantic content (what it means) and emotional content (how you feel about it). Connotation issues reveal emotional content. So do tone of voice, body language, and timing of the message. If the emotional content is not appropriately selected, then the semantic content may go unnoticed or be rejected outright, even if it's reasonable on the face of it: "If he told me the sun rose in the east, I wouldn't believe him!" To avoid problems in this area, set goals as a prelude to communication. All communication is designed to change: 1) an attitude or feeling (persuasive), 2) a level of knowledge (informational), 3) what someone does (behavioral), or a combination of the three. When you decide what you want to happen as a result of your communication, you will find it much easier to select the communication tools and approaches that are most likely to achieve the results that you want.

Stage 2: From Transmission to the Recipient

In any form of communication, there is at least the potential for information loss and information distortion through the process of transmission. To minimize loss and distortion, you need to identify those factors that can cause it and determine appropriate strategies to compensate.

Medium. The first decision that you need to make is the transmission medium. Should you have a face-to-face conversation with the recipient, or will the telephone be sufficient? Do you need a formal meeting, or can you catch the person walking down the hall? Would voice mail be OK? You could communicate in writing or by letter, memo, fax, or email. Each gives a different feeling and has different strengths and weaknesses. Is this communication for a single individual or for a group? If it's for a group, should the group be notified together or separately? (What about gossip?) Generally it's better to have high-emotion-content communication in person and privately, and communication with a high degree of precision and detail in writing. Issues of physical location and speed requirements (not to mention expense) can force use of media such as telephones and voice mail, even when not ideal. You may also use a combination approach (initial discussion in person with a follow-up in writing to confirm what was said and decided).

Noise and distractions. It's often recommended that discussions of substance not be held in a public setting, not only because of possible emotional and privacy issues, but also because of the high probability of distractions and interruptions. Noise can be literal (a loud discussion in the next cubicle, ringing telephones, music, construction work) or symbolic (frequent interruptions even if environmentally silent). Distractions are a form of noise in terms of interference with the communications process.

Stage 3: From Language to Thought

Once the communication passes through the environment to the receiver, other factors come into play.

Perceptions. Albert Mehrabian's classic study indicates that three elements influence the listener's perception and decoding of a message: words, 7 percent; voice/tone, 38 percent; facial expression, 55 percent (Carr-Ruffino 1993, 181). "I'm glad you're here," can be said with a smile and an enthusiastic voice, or with a frown and a voice dripping with sarcasm. The semantic content remains the same, but the perception and reaction will be vastly different.

Assumptions, past experience, and preconceptions. If someone thinks that you're a jerk, then everything you say will be run through his *jerk filter,* and few of us escape unscathed. It's vital that you know how people perceive you and how they experience their relationships with you on the grounds that they will always filter and interpret your communication based on those notions, whether or not they are fair and accurate. You may need to adjust your approach as a result.

Interpretation. Not only are the words that you used interpreted in terms of their denotative meaning, but they are also interpreted based on their connotations for the listener. In addition to general connotations, people may add connotations to your speech based on their ideas about you.

Stage 4: Feedback and Verification

With all that can go wrong in the process, perhaps it's not surprising how widespread poor communication is. Maybe it's more surprising that anyone ever understands anything!

In communications engineering, it's important to have feedback to verify that the desired message was transmitted. In your communication, you need to verify three things, as follows.

Was the message received? In non-immediate communications such as voice mail and correspondence, you may need to verify that the message was received. Even in immediate dialogue, a person may have been daydreaming or had her mind elsewhere when you were speaking.

Was the message understood? Especially if the message that you are delivering is subject to disagreement or rejection, it's important to distinguish between understanding and agreement. In a disciplinary conversation, for example, it's often customary for the supervisor to have the employee sign an acknowledgment that certain rules were explained. This doesn't mean that the employee necessarily agrees with those rules; but it confirms and records the idea of understanding.

Was the message accepted? At this level, you are looking for agreement to the communication. It's often important to make agreement explicit and, in certain situations, able to be confirmed later. (Put it in writing.)

How to Give and Get Feedback

The classic model for communications feedback is to accept full personal responsibility for the communication by using phrases such as: "Let me see if I understand what you said. If I understand correctly, you said. … " and then repeat or paraphrase the content. The recipient has the choice of saying, "Yes, you understand," or, "No, that's not what I said." In the latter case, don't argue. Apologize and try again: "I'm sorry. I must have misunderstood. Why don't you try it again?" By accepting responsibility, you defuse the situation and move closer to the goal. This is paraphrasing, and communications experts are virtually unanimous in recommending it.

When you are communicating and need feedback from the other party, say it like this: "I need to make sure I'm expressing myself properly. It would help me if you said back to me what you heard me say, so I can make sure I said it well." When the information is repeated, you can say, "Yes, you understood. Thank you," or, "I must not have communicated well. Let me try again." Accept responsibility again so that you defuse the situation and move ahead.

You'll frequently hear the term *one-way communication*. This model helps you realize that there is no such thing as one-way communication. There's two-way and no-way, but nothing in between.

Listening ... and Being Quiet

Sometimes, the best communications strategy is to say ... nothing. Listening defuses anger, validates people, and sometimes gets more accomplished. Negotiation adviser David Steibel says, "The error is thinking better or more communication is the answer. Sometimes the strategy that is necessary in solving the business problem is to stop and regroup" (Weldon 1997, 7).

Effective listening skills include not only concentrating on what the person has to say, but also on using the appropriate body language, such as eye contact (but not the staring contest!), leaning forward, nodding your head, and paraphrasing what you've heard. It is, by the way, perfectly acceptable to take notes while listening to important or detailed information, as long as you keep eye contact while doing so.

Exercise 10

Communications Effectiveness

A good way to improve communications effectiveness is to monitor and debrief actual situations. Over the next two weeks, identify communications that went particularly well or particularly poorly. Using the model and description discussed, identify reasons why it went well or poorly, and ways that you might have handled it better.

Some Communications That Went Well

Date _____ Person(s) _____

Situation _____
_____

Reasons Why It Went Well _____
_____
_____

Ways It Might Have Gone Even Better _____
_____
_____
_____

Date _____ Person(s) _____

Situation _____
_____

Reasons Why It Went Well _____
_____
_____

Ways It Might Have Gone Even Better _____
_____
_____
_____

Date _____ Person(s) _____

Situation _____
_____

Reasons Why It Went Well _____
_____
_____

Ways It Might Have Gone Even Better _____
_____
_____
_____

Date _____ Person(s) _____

Situation _____
_____

Reasons Why It Went Well _____
_____
_____

Ways It Might Have Gone Even Better _____
_____
_____
_____

Some Communications That Went Poorly

Date _____ Person(s) _____

Situation _____
_____

Reasons Why It Went Poorly _____
_____
_____

Ways It Might Have Gone Better _____
_____
_____
_____

Date _____ Person(s) _____

Situation _____
_____

Reasons Why It Went Poorly _____
_____
_____

Ways It Might Have Gone Better _____
_____
_____
_____

Date _____ Person(s) _____

Situation _____
_____

Reasons Why It Went Poorly _____
_____
_____

Ways It Might Have Gone Better _____
_____
_____
_____

Date _____   Person(s) _____

Situation _____
_____

Reasons Why It Went Poorly _____
_____
_____

Ways It Might Have Gone Better _____
_____
_____
_____

Debrief of Exercise 10

Peters once observed, "If a job's worth doing, it's worth doing badly" (Peters and Tracy 1989). While that's not what you were probably taught, there are two important truths in the statement. The first involves the realization that the way most people get good at most tasks is to start badly and work up—practice. The second truth is this: if you have a choice between doing a good job or a bad job, then you pick the good job. But sometimes your choice is between a bad job and doing nothing—in which case sometimes the bad job is strongly preferable.

In developing communications skills, both truths are important. The first is that improvement comes from practice and feedback, and this exercise provides a regular feedback mechanism. In fact, you should return to this exercise whenever a communication goes particularly well or particularly badly. The second is that communication is an inherently imperfect process, but when the alternative is a complete lack of communication, that may well be worse.

Communication and Technical Professionals

The basics of effective communication are the same for anyone, and even in a management role in a technical environment you will still need to communicate with many people other than technical professionals. There are, however, a few communications issues special to your situation.

Open Communication/Information Flow

Technical professionals have a high need for relevant information, and also require the opportunity to offer feedback and to participate in the decision process. "Thoroughly informed professionals," observes Watts Humphrey, "invariably have many ideas on what to do and how to do it" (1997, 176). Avoid the *mushroom syndrome* discussed earlier, in which you keep people in the dark. Your credibility as a manager is strongly influenced by the degree to which your communication is perceived as honest. While there is information that you cannot share with your team, work to ensure that it is the exception, not the rule.

Goal-Oriented Communication

Technical teams that don't receive good information about management goals and directions tend naturally to go in their own directions, which is based on fascination with the work and desire for technical excellence and innovation—whether or not that ultimately translates into customer-focused goals.

One-Up/One-Down

Linguist Deborah Tannen identified a key pattern in certain communication: "When you offer information, the information itself is the message. But the fact that you have the information, and the person you are speaking to doesn't, also sends a metamessage of superiority" (1990, 62). Scott Adams explains that engineers have a rational objective for social interaction: "Demonstrate mental superiority and mastery of all subjects" (1996, 174). Watch for your own possible tendencies in this area and for the sensitivity that you may find in some of your team members to any communication in which they may perceive themselves to be less than completely expert.

Notes

1. An excellent discussion of connotation and denotation can be found in Stone and Bell 1972, 98–101.
2. Obfuscatory: Indistinct, confusing, obscure. Prolix: Wordy and tedious. Sesquipedalian: Given to using long words (from the Latin, of a foot and a half in length).

Chapter 7
Management and Supervisory Skills

The Work of Supervisors and Managers

You may have suspected this all along: Supervisors and managers don't work, at least not in the same sense of the word as staff members work. The *work* of management isn't about actually accomplishing the projects yourself, but about helping others to do so, while taking care of planning, coordination, oversight, and staff development yourself.

You may find yourself, especially if new to a leadership or management position, in the position of being a *working supervisor* or *working project manager*. In that role, you are expected to perform certain of the technical tasks personally, while also providing leadership and guidance to others in coordinating the overall work. This calls for careful balance of your different responsibilities and one important caution: it's not a good idea to assign the most difficult and challenging tasks to yourself, because you have this other role to perform. And make no mistake: it's the management role, not the technical role, on which you will be evaluated for future promotions.

The famous acronym POSDIC describes a manager's responsibilities (Towers 1993, 44):

Plan
Organize
Staff
Direct
Inspect
Control

As a manager, you must work on managerial tasks. In this section, you'll focus on what you must do to succeed in your management role.

Delegation

The failure to delegate is a key reason why managers fail. There are both technical and emotional obstacles to delegation that you must recognize and overcome in order to be successful.

Rules for Effective Delegation

1. **Explain the task specifically and thoroughly**. Make sure that team members know what they are expected to do, what the deadline is, how the result will be evaluated, what problems they might expect, and what resources they have. Use feedback to ensure that communication has taken place.
2. **Encourage feedback about concerns and questions**. Good listening makes successful delegation far more likely. Encourage questions, ideas, and feedback. You don't necessarily have to agree with every objection that a team member may raise, but it's important to know what those objections are.
3. **Explain background and benefits**. For most people, and technical professionals specifically, the *why* question is a key to effective delegation. Technical professionals often find it difficult to do a job if they think that it's pointless.
4. **Give clear authority to match responsibility**. A good model for communicating authority is to determine the dividing line between three types of issues:
   a. "You decide." These issues are ones that the team member decides and acts without the need to check with you.
   b. "You decide, but run it past me." More complex issues, significant expenditures, and policy matters may need your approval, or at least awareness. At this level, the team member still makes the decision, but needs your sign-off to go ahead. Generally, you should agree unless you have a specific reason to disagree.
   c. "Bring it to me, and I'll decide." There are always limits to any grant of authority. Expenditures over a certain level, policy decisions with precedent-setting implications, and decisions that may have political impact in the organization are all areas where it may be necessary for you to keep authority.
5. **Let delegatees do it their way—and don't hover**. You may have experienced someone who delegated tasks to you but stood over your shoulder the whole time, commenting and criticizing. The strong temptation is to *go limp*, to allow him to take control and not take the delegation. This behavior happens for many reasons, including insecurity, perfectionism, or distrust of the employee. Whatever the reason, if you are subject to this behavior, work to overcome it. If the reason is distrust of the subordinate, start with simple, brief tasks, then gradually increase the scope of assignments (Brown and Dudley 1989, 14).
6. **Use interim deadlines or checkpoints as necessary**. For large projects, employee development, and problem avoidance, design your delegations with interim deadlines or checkpoints to ensure that the work is coming along properly.
7. **Be available for feedback and coaching**. Depending on the temperament and style of the subordinate, you can be available either on her timetable ("If you need anything, just whistle") or by scheduled appointment ("We'll meet each Thursday afternoon for a progress update").
8. **Provide feedback and recognition for accomplishment**. As the old saying goes, "the opposite of love is not hate; rather it is indifference." The very worst thing that you can do is not to criticize someone's performance; rather it is to ignore him. For the sake of delegation, morale, and motivation, recognize all work done—praising that done well, and helping to improve that which needs improving.

Exercise 11

Do You Have a Delegation Problem?

Answer "Yes" or "No" to each question:

_____ Do you regularly take work home?

_____ Do you work longer hours than your team members and others in your organization?

_____ Do you often have to do things that others should be doing by themselves?

_____ When you look at a task, do you seldom (if ever) think to ask yourself, "Could a team member do this task for me?"

_____ When you return from an absence, is your in basket usually overflowing?

_____ Do you lack confidence in some of your team members?

_____ Do you think some of your team members are lazy and unmotivated?

_____ Do your team members complain that it's hard to get time with you to discuss assignments?

_____ Are you still handling some of the same activities and problems that you did before your last promotion?

_____ Are you constantly interrupted by questions for guidance from people who work for you?

_____ Do you enjoy _keeping your finger in every pot_?

_____ Are you always in a rush to meet every deadline?

_____ Are you finding yourself increasingly unable to keep on top of priorities?

Debrief of Exercise 11

Generally, five or more "yes" answers are symptomatic of a delegation problem. As the questions in this exercise show, the overworked and harried boss is often a poor delegator at heart. While effective delegation is a challenge (often one of the hardest challenges that new managers face), it's necessary for you to cope with your other responsibilities.

There are two different reasons to delegate, and the approach and methods that you use depend on the reason. The first reason to delegate is to free time for yourself to do those things that you can't delegate. The second reason to delegate is to provide on-the-job training and coaching to help your team members grow and advance. (These are known as _developmental assignments_.)

Obstacles to Delegation

There are two primary sets of obstacles to effective delegation: overload or resistance on the part of the delegatee, and resistance to the act of delegation on the part of the delegator.

Why do managers have trouble delegating? The foremost reason is the "I can do it better myself" syndrome. Of course, that's often true. You can do it better yourself. You probably have the experience and the skill—and this may be why you were promoted in the first place. The next reason is, "It's easier if I do it." No flak, it's done exactly as you prefer, and it's probably done quicker.

Those reasons are valid if and only if you're looking at the situation from a short-term perspective. It does take time to train, and you will get resistance and some task failure. However, in the long run, effective delegation is the best tool that you have to develop your team members, increase overall productivity—and qualify yourself for your next promotion.

Why do team members resist delegation? Sometimes it's them; other times it may be you.

Them issues include insecurity about individuals' abilities to master a new skill, fear of consequences of not getting it right the first time, fear of awkwardness in the learning stage, dislike of the job assignment itself, or feeling that successful performance will not advance in the desired career direction. Possible solutions include emotional reassurance and support, detailed coaching, explanation of benefits and payoffs from the employee's point of view, and making sure that unpleasant or boring assignments are fairly rotated among subordinates.

You issues include perfectionism, impatience, patronization, unavailability for information or feedback, lack of feedback, unclear instructions, brusque delivery, and micromanagement. If you continually get resistance to your delegation from multiple team members, the likelihood is that you are contributing to your own problems. Get feedback on your delegation style, and work on improving your techniques.

What You Cannot Delegate

Management expert Mark Towers provides the following list of work that you cannot delegate, although in some cases it's possible to share or invite participation in these activities (1993, 47–48):

- Long-range planning
- Selection of key players on your team
- Monitoring key projects or key functions
- Motivating fellow team members
- Evaluating team members
- Rewarding team members
- Participating in rituals and special events
- Personal matters
- Sensitive matters
- Precedent-setting matters.

In addition, you can't delegate responsibility for disciplining team members, matters involving confidential information, or work that is legally restricted in its performance (certain legal or medical tasks, for example).

Delegation Issues in Supervising Technical Professionals

Expect a greater degree of negotiation and justification when you are delegating to technical professionals, who often have 1) their own sense of priorities, which may conflict with yours, and 2) a strong need to know *why* about almost everything.

Watch for conflict between the technical professional desire to do the work in a way that is technically excellent and the organizational or customer goal to get it done by Tuesday. It's not enough to delegate the work assignment; you must put it in an appropriate context so that the delegatee understands the context and the real goal.

If you are a working supervisor, beware of the *hero syndrome*, or taking on the toughest technical challenges yourself. Not only does this lead to overload and potential burnout on your part, but it also stifles staff development.

If your role is not to perform technical work yourself, you still need to keep your own skills high so that you can offer advice and support, and you can keep the respect of your team members.

Recruiting and Staffing

Recruiting and hiring, both from the outside and within the organization, as well as staffing (proposing and justifying team levels, writing job descriptions, conducting performance appraisals, and so on), are other key elements of a management role.

Recruiting and Hiring

Whether you are permitted to hire on your own or must follow specific organizational steps and policies (especially true if you are a manager in a government agency), it's always a good idea to consult with your human resources department, your own supervisor, and others to help you with the hiring process. This is true especially if recruiting and hiring is new to you. Consultant Marlene Caroselli, Ed.D., recommends six steps to prepare for hiring, as featured in the sidebar.

Recruiting Issues for Technical Professionals

Because in the real world credentials often take second place to actual ability, you have to figure whether the technical professional has the real ability to do the job. At Microsoft, for example, an interview focus is to see if the applicant can do structured problem solving. Microsoft President Steve Ballmer used to use this exercise a lot (he switched to new puzzles because the word got out): "I'd ask people to pick a number between one and a hundred. You get [the answer I picked] on the first guess, I give you five bucks ... I tell you high, low on your guess. Takes you two guesses, I give you four. Three, two, one, zero. Then you pay me a buck, you pay me two. Do you want to play or not" (1)?

If you use tests of any sort, make sure that you clear them with the human resources department. Tests must be fair, nondiscriminatory, and based on actual job requirements.

Staffing

Staffing issues can take an enormous amount of your time as a supervisor and manager, but the quality of your efforts in this area strongly impacts your results. The first tip is to develop contacts and relationships with the human resources department, which may be able to provide resources, ranging from books and formats to actually performing some of the work for you. (Some human resources departments draft job descriptions and will even perform a *desk audit* of a position to help determine the critical job elements.)

One of the hardest things to do is to get authorization for putting additional people on your team. It's usually much easier to obtain permission to purchase equipment and supplies. Management consultant George Fuller recommends structuring an overall campaign to get additional help (1995, 287–90). First, drop casual hints with your boss to prepare the way. Expect to get a negative answer, but probe for underlying reasons and issues. Research a comprehensive justification, remembering that decisions to expand staffing levels are normally made and approved at the highest levels of the organization—your boss may not be able to say yes even if he agrees with you. Ultimately, you must be able to demonstrate—with hard facts and evidence—that hiring someone will benefit the company from a profit-and-loss standpoint. The company must gain more than it costs to hire the new employee, and don't forget indirect salary costs, such as benefits. Prepare spreadsheets showing financial benefits of the proposed increase. Even if you don't always get what you want (and you won't), a properly presented and defended business case will enhance your reputation in the eyes of senior management, which will be an asset for future requests.

Six Steps for Better Hiring

1. **Decide how you will find the person to fill the position.** Think about internal versus external recruiting, participation of human resources, and use of contacts and networks. Make sure that you are in compliance with Affirmative Action and other regulations and policies.

2. **Determine the qualities and skills that you wish the candidate to have**; then revise, update, or create a job description. A well-written job description (unfortunately a rarity in many organizations) can be a real management asset. The first goal is to determine the essential (as opposed to marginal) functions of the job, then determine the requirements and qualifications that someone would need in order to fulfill the job. Write an honest and accurate job description that focuses on those essentials, and you'll often have some of your interview questions done for you. What personality traits are important? If it is a high-team job, interpersonal skills are important, but if the work is highly solitary and individual in nature, then the successful candidate must enjoy that sort of environment. If you're hiring to replace an existing team member, consult with that person on job characteristics and skills that are important.

3. **Prepare a list of questions that you will ask of each interview candidate.** W. R. Ernisse, a vice president of Xerox, says, "Too often, most of the interview time is spent with the manager describing the open job versus finding out about the applicants" (Caroselli 1993, 9). Don't make that mistake. There is certainly a need for the applicant to ask questions and learn about the job, but your focus needs, at least initially, to be on learning about the candidate. (Marlene Caroselli has an extensive list in her book (1993); often your human resource department will have a list of interview questions from which you can work.) You might want to review your questions with human resources to ensure that you aren't asking anything prohibited by law.

4. **Take notes during the interview; prepare a form to keep information in a usable format.** A good skill to learn is taking notes while maintaining eye contact with the individual. Make notetaking a background activity. This is progressively important with the more applicants that you are interviewing for the position.

5. **Choose an interview style.** Chatty, scripted, hypothetical (what would you do if. …), hidden agenda (observe for characteristics and reactions not implicit in the questions that you ask), benchmarking against an ideal candidate—all are techniques used. Some interviewers prefer a "let's get to know each other" style, others a hard-hitting *inquisition* format.

6. **Develop a definite plan for the interview.** Just as an agenda is critical for a good meeting, think about the stages and actions in the interview so that it works well for both you and the applicant.

Source: Caroselli 1993, 10–29

Staffing Issues for Technical Professionals

Staffing and recruiting of technical professionals often runs afoul of the law of supply and demand, especially when your needs are highly specialized. It's a good idea to do a little market research in advance of staffing needs (again, get your human resources department to help you) so that you'll know the going rates and demand.

Getting the best help isn't merely a matter of paying the best money. The best technical professionals want to work in an environment that supports their aspirations, whether for skill growth, freedom to experiment, working with the latest and greatest equipment, doing projects on the cutting edge, or a relaxed or nonexistent dress code. If your environment isn't attractive to top talent, it's time to change it. Remember, if you build it, they will come.

Performance Appraisals

Performance appraisals are often the bane of supervisors, and in many organizations the process is essentially an empty one. You can, however, make the appraisal process beneficial. "The key to making performance appraisals worthwhile," observe Jerry Brown and Denise Dudley, "is transforming them from a one-way evaluation into a two-way discussion" [1989, 30]. (The currently popular 360-degree evaluation mechanism, when properly executed, is extremely helpful in this regard.)

Several weeks before the scheduled appraisal, let team members know that the appraisals are coming up. Encourage them to prepare a list of their major accomplishments for the past work period and their own ideas for improvement. Make sure that you deliberately ask about positive contributions and barriers that might keep people from doing their best work.

Prepare in advance with your own observations and comments, making sure that you identify and emphasize positive accomplishments and progress that you have witnessed. Of course, do identify desired areas for improvement, but ensure that you discuss them in behavioral terms—specific and measurable so that people know what you expect.

Write the appraisal after the meeting, considering what you learned as well as what you shared. Listen to comments and feedback from the team member, but make changes only if you agree with her. Ultimately, the appraisal must reflect your own best judgment.

The annual performance appraisal process has some inherent limitations, the most important being that if you haven't given people performance feedback regularly, once a year is too little and too late. Let your appraisal process serve as an evaluation of your own performance as a manager; while an employee may disagree with your evaluation, an employee should never be surprised to learn what you think. That's evidence that you haven't provided sufficient feedback all year long.

Performance Appraisal Issues for Technical Professionals

If the appraisal process appears to be more useless management foofaraw, expect to get disdain from your technical staff. If raises and bonuses are tied to it, expect to get flak about whatever elements your technical staff doesn't perceive as valid: "What do you mean my attendance was only *satisfactory*? Who cares if I come in at eight sharp? I get ten times more work done than anybody else, and I don't think you have any business even paying attention to this!"

Although you may have to use a performance appraisal system implemented by management that may not be responsive to your needs (this may be particularly true if you are in a technical group in a nontech organization), you can always develop your own appraisal system tied into meaningful and job-related issues. Use it with your staff, then map the *real* performance appraisal onto the *official* document, helping people to understand that their ratings are based on mutually negotiated performance objectives that are clearly relevant to the job that needs to be done.

Training

Your role as a manager includes responsibility for formal (classroom and outside) as well as informal (usually on-the-job) training and development of team members.

With over $200 billion a year spent in formal and informal employee education and training, it's vital for all levels of management in the organization—not just human resource professionals and trainers—to understand how to make training work in building productive teams.

What Training Does—and Doesn't Do

Training all by itself is useless. Training only delivers results when it's made part of an overall strategy. You must first identify the target results—the changes that you want in behavior, knowledge, and attitude. You must look at the reasons for current levels—is it the person, the system, or the nature of the work? Training can solve some organizational problems, but not others. Before turning to training to solve a problem, first identify whether the barriers to productivity can be better removed some other way.

Training Issues for Technical Professionals

The dichotomy between *hard-skill* and *soft-skill* training often takes on particular power when training technical professionals. You may find that it's easier for them to see the value in hard-skill training, and to reject any possible value in soft-skill training—especially if it is in fact in an area in which their behavior is deficient. They see being sent to a communications or team-building seminar as implicit criticism, which, of course, it often is.

To overcome this objection, structure training as part of an overall program of evaluation, assessment, and staff development. Lay a foundation for soft-skill courses by identifying in behavioral terms problem issues that your team member may have. Work to get buy-in and acceptance that a problem exists before shipping the person off to training. If not, the person will attend the training, turn off any information in advance, annoy the trainer and other participants, and waste the money and time that you spent.

Notice that training can often be structured as a reward and motivator, especially if it's on a cutting-edge topic in which a team member has an interest. Even if the training can't be fully justified as immediately job related, many organizations have learned that the topic being studied is often less important than the fact of learning—send her.

Motivation and Behavior Modification

Motivation expert Barbara Fielder says, "The good news is that everyone is motivated. The bad news is that you can't personally motivate anyone. ... People do things for their own reasons—not yours" (1996, 5).

What Motivation Is

Have you ever met an unmotivated person? Most managers say yes—emphatically. However, think of it this way: Have you ever met a worker who spent more time and energy scheming to get out of the work than it would have taken just to do it and get it over with? Probably you have. Is this person unmotivated? Absolutely not. This person is highly motivated—just in a different direction than you would prefer.

Therefore, if someone isn't doing what you want, there are three possible reasons, each with its own strategy:

Don't Know
Can't Do
Won't Do

To change the behavior of an individual or a group, you need to first figure which of these three reasons applies, and then develop a strategy to change the conditions. As the legendary Dale Carnegie observed, "The only way I can get you to do anything is by giving you what you want" (Fielder 1996, 10).

Don't-know *problem*. Obviously if someone doesn't know what you want, it's unlikely that he will do it, given that so few people are genuinely telepathic. This is why effective communications is critical to any management, supervisory, or leadership role. More problems are *don't-know* than most supervisors assume. In any event, from a tactical point of view, always begin any problem-solving approach by assuming it's a don't-know and move up from there.

Can't-do *problem*. Could the person do it if her life depended on it? If the answer is no, then it's a genuine *can't-do* problem. Possible solutions include training in the necessary skills, tools, and equipment necessary to perform the job, redesign or rethinking of the job itself, or changing the person.

Won't-do *problem*. If someone knows what you want, has the ability to do what you want, and doesn't do what you want, it must be a matter of choice. The person won't do what you want. In order to change the behavior, you need to know why the person won't do what you want. There are three categories of reasons, as shown in Case Studies 7, 8, and 9.

The answers to the questions in the case studies, unfortunately, are self-explanatory, and you have probably seen similar situations in action.

Rewards and punishments are part of behavior modification and motivation, but the first rule is to remember that the perception of the individual at the other end determines whether something is indeed a reward or a punishment.

Maslow and Herzberg

Motivational theory in the workplace owes most to two researchers: Abraham Maslow (1954) and Frederick Herzberg (1959).

Maslow's Hierarchy of Needs tells us that we tend to take action to satisfy our individual needs. Whatever need is strongest at any given time motivates us to take that action. A need motivates us as long as it is not satisfied; when satisfied, it no longer motivates us. Human needs can be shown as a series of levels, a hierarchy arranged by order of importance (see Figure 6).

The first two levels of the Hierarchy of Needs—Physiological and Safety—are usually not at issue in managing technical professionals. Basic human needs such as food, clothing, and shelter motivate people only when they don't have them and find it difficult to get them. Safety and security needs (removing of physical dangers from the environment, for example) come into play only in such situations as dramatic downsizing, in which people are afraid for their jobs.

Social needs, the need to belong and experience closeness and group affiliation, do play an important role in some technical organizations, at least with some people. You need to pay

Case Study 7

Performance Is Punished

Juanita agreed, with reservations, to develop an accounts-payable aging program for the finance department. The deadline was too tight, and the performance standards kept escalating. Her manager wasn't sympathetic to her warnings. Because she was a loyal team player, she worked overtime every night for three weeks and got the system up and running.

The result? The finance department complained that she didn't add three reports that it needed—and for which it hadn't asked. Her boss explained that she needed to spend more time discovering customer needs.

"We're a quality- and customer-focused organization," he said in his most patronizing voice.

When she told him about all of her hard work and the uncompensated overtime, his response was, "Well, you got it done, and if you learn to manage your time better, it won't be so difficult for you next time."

Question: Will Juanita work that hard on her next assignment?

Case Study 8

Failure Is Rewarded

Andrew and Mary are competing for engineering job assignments in their department. One assignment is an easy project with high visibility and little technical challenge. The other project is actually more important to the organization, but it's difficult and so technically obscure that senior management won't even be aware that it was done. They'll only know if it wasn't done.

The official mission and vision of the organization talks about rewarding people who help the organization to achieve its goals. In practice those who are visible are rewarded; those who aren't are passed over.

The person who does the easy and less important assignment will gain credit and visibility. The person who does the harder and more important assignment won't.

Question: Are Andrew and Mary going to be rewarded for success—or for failure? What will this do to their competition, and what will it do to future behavior?

Case Study 9

Performance Doesn't Matter

Wang, an outstanding programmer, has achieved his results ahead of deadline and above specification on every project for an entire year—a record unequaled by any other programmer in the department.

The management decision is to reward people based only on team performance. Everyone in the programming group gets exactly the same raise regardless of individual effort.

Question: How long before Wang goes where his work will be appreciated and valued?

---

attention to how much individuals need a sense of inclusion, and modify your supervisory and communication styles to help meet that need. You also may need to monitor the attempt by some teams to ostracize certain individuals. It may be necessary to work with the ostracized individual to modify his behaviors, with the team members to get them to stop excluding members, or both.

Your primary motivation efforts need to be directed at Levels 4 and 5. At the Esteem level, people's needs are to be recognized for their special contributions. Many management systems are built around the importance of recognition and praise as motivators. Research indicates that the number-one thing that employees want is recognition: verbal praise, a note, a public announcement, or positive feedback through the performance appraisal process (Fielder 1996, 18).

As a manager of technical professionals, however, you may have already found yourself baffled when your sincere, heartfelt praise is rejected or ignored by some team members. First, remember that different people value being praised for different things. Praising a Visionary Leader (NT) for a routine task well done is not only irrelevant, but may also even produce suspicion. Worse, this kind of person also judges the praise-giver in deciding what reaction to take toward the praise, and generally has trouble accepting appreciation at all (Keirsey and Bates 1984, 131).

Motivators and Dissatisfiers
Herzberg's motivation model distinguishes between motivators and "dissatisfiers," or "hygiene" factors. Motivators contribute to job satisfaction, but dissatisfiers and hygiene factors can only demotivate if not present.

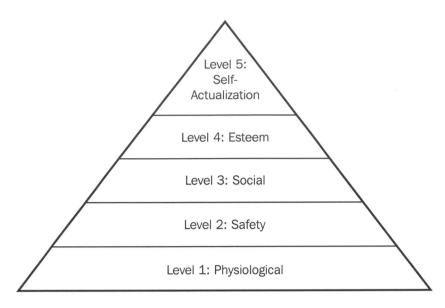

Figure 6   Maslow's Hierarchy of Needs

Herzberg's Job Satisfiers

Motivators	**Hygiene Factors**
Achievement	Company Policies
Advancement	Wages and Benefits
Recognition	Work Relationships
Challenge	Working Conditions

The tie-in between Herzberg and Maslow is that only those elements that fit Levels 4 and 5 of the hierarchy provide long-term motivating effects. Factors in Levels 1, 2, and 3, once satisfied, no longer motivate.

The one that surprises most people is Wages and Benefits. Remember that many people gain immense job satisfaction from nonprofit or academic work that pays much less than a private sector equivalent. Once basic needs are met, other factors come into play. The important question is this: Do you feel fairly compensated for the level of work and responsibility that you have? If the answer is yes, then feeling overpaid doesn't make people work harder.

Your approach to motivation needs to be rooted in these concepts. You need to identify the ways in which people gain Levels 4 and 5 satisfaction and work to increase them, while working to remove negative elements that pull people into the lower levels of the hierarchy.

Remember as well that motivation is an issue only at the won't-do level. All the motivation in the world can't overcome a don't-know or can't-do issue.

Motivation Issues for Technical Professionals

Technical management consultant Dr. Richard J. Stein points out that technical people have unusual motivations—sometimes so remote as to be incomprehensible. Technical professionals may work amazing numbers of hours fueled only by sugar, caffeine, and pizza, and the motivation obviously isn't money, approval of peers, promotion, or any normal reason (Stein 1993, 98–100).

Stein identifies four special rules for motivation that are particularly powerful when it comes to technical professionals:

- Your own credibility is key—explain what motivates you.
- Utilize the power of the group norm—once you get the majority headed in the right direction, it might catch on.
- Emphasize the temporary nature of the duller work.
- Talk—and listen—to people about their motivation, projects they've enjoyed, and goals that they have.

Software development expert Watts S. Humphrey emphasizes focusing on output and giving professional discretion on how to produce it, having frequent informal meetings, making suggestions rather than giving specific directions, showing enthusiasm about good work, involving the most productive people in at least some nonproject activities, and asking the most promising professionals to present their work to managers, customers, and outside professional groups. Finally, require individuals to make plans and estimates for their own work. Ask tough and probing questions to make the estimates solid and realistic. Good people thrive on hard work, especially when their managers demand it (Humphrey 1997, 72–73).

An additional recommendation is this: Figure what's important, and focus your attention there; ignore messy offices, fashion *faux pax*, tardiness, and a certain amount of asocial behavior as long as people get the job done.

Discipline and Termination

The goal of discipline is to correct inappropriate behavior or inadequate job performance. Termination is what you do when discipline has failed. When you look at the distasteful but altogether real need to exercise discipline in the workplace, follow the nine steps outlined in the sidebar.

Make sure that you are consistent in the offenses that need discipline. Attacking a tardiness problem with one team member when you ignore tardiness of other team members will breed conflict.

Disciplining Issues for Technical Professionals

You'll find with some technical professionals that if the rule doesn't make sense, then they will not follow it, regardless of consequences. If a technical professional's skills and talents are good enough, then you may find it difficult to push the discipline to its final results, choosing to live with the problem rather than lose the person. If you suspect that is the case, try negotiating with the team member to get minimally acceptable compliance, and decide in advance what you will live with. Watch for one person's disregard of the rules to be contagious, as others may decide to push your limits as well. One way to handle this is if someone is going to get a free ride on a certain rule, the free ride has to be justified to the group by something specific that the person has done to earn the exception—then if others want the exception, they have to accomplish the same level of work.

Nine Steps to Proper Discipline

1. Initially assume that any inappropriate behavior or inadequate job performance is a don't-know problem, and conduct a private meeting to make sure that the employee knows the rules, issues, and goals. Keep handwritten documentation of the meeting, but don't put anything in the personnel file (2).

2. Verify that you don't have a can't-do problem. Consider skills, aptitudes, training, and the nature of the job and circumstances. If you discover can't-do issues, design a plan to deal with them.

3. If the behavior doesn't change, then have an informal meeting on the issues. At this point—but not before—it's appropriate to point out the consequences that might result from a lack of change.

4. Depending on the nature of the situation, meet with your manager and/or the appropriate human resources professional either just before or shortly after this meeting, especially if the meeting doesn't go productively. If it becomes necessary to formally discipline or even terminate the employee, then you will need the support of your manager. ... If you aren't going to get the support, you need to know now. You'll usually find that you can only get his support if you follow his advice.

5. Study the formal disciplinary procedures of your organization. Know the rules and any applicable laws and regulations (such as union contracts) that affect your actions. Follow them to the letter, keep written records, and ask for advice and support whenever you have any doubt.

6. At each step in the formal disciplinary process, take the action and inform the person of the next step. Never bluff. If you really won't act, don't threaten. If your own management won't back you, don't threaten.

7. Work as hard as you can to help the employee turn around the behavior or performance. Ultimately, you want to give the person a choice: change the behavior or change the employment.

8. Stay respectful and positive throughout, even in a termination meeting (3).

9. Always keep it confidential.

Conflict Management

People in an organization work in close quarters for long periods of time, often under stressful conditions. It's not surprising that friction builds and builds. Many employees spend more time with their coworkers than with their spouses or significant others—without the luxury of having chosen them in the first place!

A certain amount of irritation and friction is unavoidable, and most grownups can work out minor problems on their own. Let them. A few problems come to you for resolution. Try pushing the affected parties into negotiating their own solution. This may help avoid starting a pattern in which all petty problems come to you.

When the friction between two specific people begins to mount, the issue may be personal or professional, but it's time for you to step in. Conflict can grow into open warfare before you know it. Try the following steps.

First ask yourself a few questions. Is there a pattern of conflict between two specific individuals, a pattern of general conflict spreading throughout an entire department, or simply isolated cases of friction and flare-up? Also, is the conflict affecting work performance in some visible way? If it is not affecting work performance, let it alone.

If it's isolated friction and flare-up, then step in when the matter goes over the bounds of professional conduct, and assertively tell the people involved to work out their differences on their own and inform you of their decision.

If it's a pattern of general conflict spreading throughout an entire department, it may be one or two specific individuals who are poisoning the well, or it may be anxiety or frustration with the state of the organization. After a major downsizing, the remaining employees experience survivor's guilt. Anticipating a major downsizing can spark competitive behavior and blame shifting in a perverse game of musical chairs.

If it is conflict involving a few specific employees, the conflict can spread throughout the department. You must resolve the problem at its source or else end with a department-wide nightmare. Following are some ideas.

If the Issue Is Personal Dislike

You may be able to limit individuals' contact with each other by making changes in physical proximity or work assignments, but not to the extent that it puts extra burdens on other employees or on the quality of work. This is a situation that calls for direct, assertive statements of supervisory authority. State firmly that while there is no work rule that people need to like one another, certain conduct is unacceptable on the job—public arguments and spats, refusal to perform because "it's her job," disrupting others' work with complaining, and so on. You may have to enforce this strongly before people get the idea that you will not tolerate bad behavior, regardless of personal feelings. Try discussing with each person the performance benefits of working with the other. How does working together benefit the team? What good can come out of working more effectively together? If the organization is working with a team concept, emphasize the importance of teamwork. You may even want to send one or both to training situations that promote team-building activities.

If the Issue Is Disagreement about Work Duties

It's legitimate for employees to need guidance from their supervisors about work rules and specific duties. In fact, conflicts of this type often arise because the supervisor hasn't been sufficiently clear and specific. You can set specific duties and make work assignments, or you can list the duties and ask the affected employees to make their own choices, write them down and then tell you.

If the Issue Is Disagreement about Direction or Policy

The affected people need to be clear about legitimate versus excessive disagreement. There are always boundaries, and your challenge is to describe those boundaries in behavioral language.

If the Issue Is Real Differences in Work Performance

If you have identified that the conflict results from real differences in work performance, then you need to focus on the work performance issues in order to deal with the conflict. Plan for a developmental conference with one or both employees (depending on who has the actual performance problem). Only by resolving the performance problem can you manage the conflict issue.

If no change results from your efforts at communication, don't give up. Conflict has a strong level of emotion, not logic, and a single round of dialogue is often just not enough. Review the outcome of the first round. Look again at behavioral issues. Remember, people hating each other is not a problem—people shouting at each other, refusing to work, and interrupting you and others are problems.

You should gradually become more directive in subsequent rounds of dialogue. Assertively tell people what the ground rules are for dealing with conflict. Make it clear that you will not accept disruption of the office, failure to complete the work, or continual wasting of your time. Unless there is a clear performance issue with one employee but not the other, hold both employees equally responsible for resolving the conflict, and make it clear that any consequences for failing to resolve the conflict will fall equally on both. And follow through if necessary.

In the real world, the situation may come down to the necessity of terminating employees for the persistent inability to get along. While justice may demand that both parties be terminated because they're equally at fault, the reality may be that one person's technical skills and organizational value strongly exceed that of the other person. This is an example of the Rule of Slack—employees get cut different amounts of slack for their behavior, based on their overall contribution to the department. Make sure that you 1) explain to the rest of the staff the basis for a decision that may seem unfair on the surface and 2) consider the likelihood of repeated bad behavior on the part of someone granted slack. Regardless of the person's overall technical skill and merit, an employee can be so disruptive and negative that he may need to be terminated, regardless of the rest of the person's contribution.

Conflict Issues for Technical Professionals

Complicating the picture is that some technical professionals are deficient in social, relationship, and communications skills, and they may have the conflict because they simply don't know how to deal with it—worse, they may think any attempt to smooth communication is manipulative or worse. There may be a can't-do issue requiring training or coaching that must be handled before the actual conflict situation can be addressed. You'll need to plan on working with resistance on the part of the affected employee as to whether the behavior change is needed.

One tactic that may work for you is to describe the *soft skill* in *hard* language, putting it into a mathematical or logical framework to fit the thought pattern of the employee. Make sure that your own feedback about the communication problems isn't delivered in a negative manner; people who are insensitive to others may be almost hypersensitive themselves. According to Daniel Goleman, employees who perceived that they had been attacked personally reacted by defensiveness, excuses, evading responsibility, or stonewalling—avoiding all contact with the manager. Inept criticism was ahead of mistrust, personality struggles, and disputes over power and pay as a reason for conflict on the job (Goleman 1995, 151–52).

Legal and Regulatory Issues

As a manager, you have certain legal and regulatory duties and responsibilities, which include EEO/Affirmative Action, the Americans with Disabilities Act, sexual harassment policies, occupational safety and health matters, and various labor laws and standards.

Case Study 10

People Unclear on the Concept I

An MBA professor told this story to his marketing class:

> I used to work for a cigarette company. My job was leading a team in developing new brands. Some brands caught on; others didn't. I had to develop a budget for next year's marketing.
>
> I proposed that we would test three brands, and calculated the costs of the test. For revenue assumptions, I took a rule-of-thumb guess that one would be successful.
>
> Finance sent the budget back and said I had to tell them which one. I argued; then they finally said to make it up. So I made it up. I forecast that brands A and C would fail and B would succeed.
>
> Then I got the approved budget. They approved Test B and canceled Tests A and C.

A full discussion is beyond the scope of this book, but try the following tips:

- Make friends with someone in the human resources department to whom you can go for advice.
- If you can't become an expert on the details of all the laws and regulations, try to support the spirit of these laws with a positive attitude, and that should minimize your danger.
- Keep handwritten records (such as a work diary) on any sensitive matters to document what you actually said and did.

Finance and Budgeting

The Role of Finance

Finance is the language of senior management. Even if your job isn't primarily oriented toward finance, it's essential to understand it. Wharton professor Dr. Steven Finkler observes: "The nonfinancial manager can no longer avoid financial information. Profit statements, operating budgets, and project analyses are a constant part of the manager's day. ... Once you understand a few basics you can fight back and demand information [from accountants] that is both useful and usefully explained" (1983, xiii).

Basic accounting concepts such as assets, liabilities, debits, and credits are part of the normal dialogue within the organization. Learn the key financial statements: balance sheet, income statement, and sources and uses of cash statement. Learn how to read them. The organization's financial condition may be stated in terms of financial ratios, such as *return on investment*, *return on assets*, and *return on equity*. These terms aren't synonyms. Depreciation and inventory costing can completely turn the financial picture of the organization upside down.

Once you've got a basic handle on these concepts, start reading the business section of the paper regularly, and consider subscribing to one or more of the standard business magazines or newspapers. You'll get the executive perspective about what's going on, which will always translate into greater power, reach, and influence on your part.

Budgeting

Finkler observes, "A budget is simply a plan" (1983, 156). A good budget takes the goals of the organization and expresses them in formal and quantifiable terms. It's essential for planning, control, and evaluation.

Your budgeting process normally begins with certain parameters given to you by senior management. Your job is to look at costs and revenues and express your plan for your department or team in light of those goals.

Properly done, budgets are a positive, valuable experience. Unfortunately, that isn't always the case.

Expect a certain amount of difficulty in fitting your situation into the company's overall goals, but remember that you aren't in fact autonomous. Develop good relations with the budgeting specialists, learn to roll with the punches, and don't fight small battles.

Self-Development as a Manager

There are hardly any problems you have or will ever have that haven't been faced or solved by someone else. Management is an exhaustively studied topic, and this book is only one example. Read, listen to tapes, and watch videos to learn more about the art of management. As you develop your skills, you will advance in your career.

It's a good idea to learn about the key thinkers and names in management and supervision. One reason that you see so many references in this book is to help you know other places to look. Also take the time to learn about management thinkers such as Tom Peters, Ken Blanchard, Peter F. Drucker, Warren Bemmis, W. Edwards Deming, Philip Crosby, J. M. Juran, Peter Senge, and Marvin Weisbord. You'll run into their names often.

Remember the value of knowledge in developing your power and influence. Study not just what you need to get today's job done, but also study what will get you where you want to be tomorrow.

Exercise 12

Self-Development Checklist

1. Develop a personal knowledge chart with areas for growth.

Topic	Current Knowledge	Needed for Advancement	Where Can I Learn More?
Communication			
Delegation			
Recruiting			
Staffing			
Training			
Motivation			
Behavior Modification			
Conflict Management			
Legal and Regulatory Issues			
Finance and Budgeting			
General Management and Supervisory Skills			
Technical Skills Relevant to My Advancement			
Other Growth Areas			

2. What organizational resources (training programs, company-paid courses, tape/video libraries, and so on) exist to develop my skills?

_____

_____

_____

_____

3. With whom may I consult in the organization to help me develop my skills in these areas?

_____

_____

_____

_____

4. What are the next steps that I can take on my own?

_____

_____

_____

_____

Debrief of Exercise 12

Personal action planning is essential for your development. Remember that management is in fact a career change, and you must develop the skills and knowledge necessary for your new occupation.

It's highly desirable to revisit this exercise on a regular basis—say every six months or so. Design a plan and put it into practice, and you'll find yourself far ahead of the game.

Notes

1. No. According to Ballmer, the expected value is negative twenty-one cents.
2. Certain offenses, such as theft, violence (or threatened violence), property destruction, and so on can result in termination without warnings or second chances. These steps are designed for the more ordinary type of behavior or performance problem.
3. For additional support, see Caroselli 1993.

Chapter 8
Alphabet Soup (or Management Initiatives for Quality)

Management Philosophies

Total quality management (TQM), reengineering, ISO-9000, management by objectives, zero-based budgeting, management by wandering around, Workforce 2000—these concepts are widely praised by some and widely derided by others. Some of them may be at work in your organization. Should you be one of the praisers or one of the deriders? It all depends.

The concept of scientific management goes back to the early days of the industrial revolution. Basic concepts such as the assembly line involve not only a concept of engineering, but also a systems approach to human beings. Obviously, there are limits to such an approach. The development of management theories and models over the course of this century has been aimed toward creating a workable systems approach that integrates people, machinery, work processes, and the other elements of the workplace into a productive synthesis.

Because systems are developed by people who often also market themselves as management consultants, there is a tendency among management writers to promote the uniqueness and perfection of their own systems and to point out the weaknesses in others, even when they are structurally quite similar. In the effort to create the *latest and greatest* management model, more recycling goes on than most systems developers are eager to admit.

The good news is that these models often do build on their predecessors, using experiential data from organizations that have worked with earlier models in order to improve them. If you ignore some of the hype, you'll find a steadily increasing body of technique from which to draw in managing your technical workforce and growing your organization.

Management Fads—Threat or Menace?

As in many other areas in our society, fads and fashions sweep the business world from time to time. It's common to deride the fad approach to management, because it has obvious drawbacks. First, it tends to promote a sense of inconsistency, which can be destabilizing and disruptive to team members. Second, the fads tend to have relatively short life spans, which sometimes means a change in direction right when the earlier approach seemed ready to pay off. Third, especially with technical professionals, the fad approach may play into the preexisting suspicion that management is clueless. (Technical professionals often have a tendency to assume this, regardless of the facts. Management is considered "guilty until proven innocent." Some of this tendency is rooted in the personality types common to technical professionals, which are often typified by a sense that authority is essentially irrelevant [Keirsey and Bates 1984, 49].)

Recent research, however, demonstrates that the counterintuitive position—management fads are positive—is actually more likely to be true. Companies that eagerly embrace the newest fad, rushing headlong into it until the new *newest fad* comes along, are more likely to prosper and be successful. How can that be?

Pro Change Management

First, management that embraces change is itself more likely to be successful. Tom Peters observes, "The most important and visible outcropping of the action bias in the excellent companies is their willingness to try things out, to experiment" (Peters and Waterman Jr. 1982, 134).

Second, the success of many of these concepts is utterly dependent on the quality of the commitment that goes into them. Dr. W. Edwards Deming, the godfather of TQM, identified that problems with quality in an organization are normally the result of failures in the system. Management controls the system. Only with active management cooperation and support can the system be changed, and only with a changing system can quality be improved. He felt this so strongly that he would only work where there was a commitment from top management. When Ford Motor Company's general manager called Dr. Deming to consult on quality in 1980, Deming refused to come to Detroit unless the president of the company requested his presence (Walton 1986, 131–32)! When management supports change initiatives, those initiatives are far more likely to produce results (1).

Fustest with the Mostest

Third, there is an enormous payoff in being first. If your organization is the twenty-third in your industry to adopt a TQM initiative, no matter how successful it is, it won't give you a competitive advantage because your competitors have already been there, done that. To gain an advantage from the benefits of the new paradigms of management, you need to be first, or at least among the first.

Fourth, these constant changes produce an organization accustomed to change. If there's one thing on which all management experts agree, it is that a company's willingness and ability to change and adapt is an essential ingredient in its long-term prospects for success.

For these reasons, if you work for a committed-management, fad-oriented company, consider it a positive element and get with the program.

What's in It for Me?

If you need additional reasons, here's a personal payoff: If management has decided to go in a given direction, then people who are clearly team players and move in the same direction will likely advance their careers. People who resist will likely not advance, even if in retrospect they turn out to have been right. (Perhaps especially if they turn out to have been right.)

Here is basic information on some of the more popular initiatives, along with references in the bibliography, to enable you to learn more about them. Consider this part of your commitment to lifelong learning, and take the initiative to discover, read, and study these new concepts as they come along. Share your knowledge with technical team members, and work to help them gain the understanding that even though things may not go as smoothly and as quickly as the theory might imply, positive change can result. You, your organization, and your team will benefit.

The following discussion of current ideas in management is not exhaustive, and new models will continue to arise. Use this as a basis for understanding the fundamentals of the differing approaches to management. The models are listed in alphabetical order.

Business Process Reengineering

Reengineering, still a fairly hot topic as of this writing, originated in the late 1980s. It was first widely promoted in 1993 by Michael Hammer and James Champy in their best-selling book, *Reengineering the Corporation*. Many of the techniques in reengineering have their roots in TQM philosophies, but deal with a perceived problem in the TQM efforts of continuous process improvement.

As management thinking has moved from an industrial model to a more cybernetic model—part of the impact of technological change—TQM has often in practice been about constant incremental improvement in existing work processes. Those work processes were often created using an industrial or manufacturing paradigm, and automating them meant using information technology to simulate old practices. Hammer wrote an influential article urging management to "obliterate, don't automate" (Hammer and Champy 1993). In other words, rather than follow a model of incremental improvement within an old paradigm, it was better to rethink processes from the ground up and reinvent them from scratch, hence *reengineering* or *business process reengineering* (BPR) [Carr and Johansson 1995, 4–7].

Given the argument about the value of leading the fad pack, many organizations that had been deeply involved in TQM began to move into a reengineering model. The reengineering approach rests on several assumptions, as shown in the sidebar, *Reengineering Fundamentals*.

Because BPR in many ways shares a TQM foundation, it's not surprising that experts David Carr and Henry Johanssen observe that companies "that get the best results from BPR have in place or have been through a rigorous TQM program" (1995, 15).

The arguments against BPR are that it is either warmed-over TQM or that its criticisms of the limits of TQM are based on a poor understanding or poor implementation of TQM. Juran Institute scholar Jeremy Main says:

> TQM does in fact achieve breakthroughs and massive, rapid change. Juran points out that successful companies "undertake quality improvements at a revolutionary pace." … TQM is hard on an organization, reengineering is even harder. With TQM you have a chance to bring the organization along and win support; with reengineering you throw the organization into a new format and hope the support will follow (1994, 310).

Excellence Model (Peters/Waterman)

Peters and Robert Waterman identified eight core principles and behaviors exhibited by "excellent" companies, which were selected by criteria such as market share, financial standing, and growth (see sidebar, *Eight Elements of the Excellent Company*).

Reengineering Fundamentals

Competitiveness. While TQM was often perceived as being primarily about an organization's internal results, BPR is primarily about competitive position. It is not about cost cutting, although that is often a side benefit.

Process focus on core business processes. The TQM emphasis on process improvement translates into BPR, but the focus is on those processes that directly touch customers and suppliers, rather than on those that are completely internal. Your strategy is to identify critical processes at which you must excel to match or beat the competition.

Radical change. The BPR approach is to go back to ground zero, to reconstruct the entire organization focused on today and tomorrow's business problems. The objective is competitiveness, not radical change for its own sake; new concepts and new ideas require new ways of doing business, not simply improving old ways of doing business.

Dramatic improvement. The commitment to a BPR approach involves setting major goals for rapid, dramatic improvement. By selecting the most important core business processes, a reengineering effort looks to equal or leapfrog the competition quickly. This is often possible because of the greater focus on information technology and other technology as enablers.

ISO-9000

ISO-9000 is a registration that an organization can earn by meeting a set of international standards on quality management and quality assurance. ISO is the International Organization for Standardization, with representatives from ninety-one countries, who develop standards, testing, and certification to encourage the trade of goods and services. The American National Standards Institute is the United States (U.S.) representative to ISO.

ISO-9000 specifies requirements for quality systems, defined in ISO Standard 8402 as: "The organizational structure, responsibilities, procedures, processes, and resources needed to implement quality management." It is a formal way to measure a TQM program (Hutchins 1993).

There are actually five international standards that an organization can choose to pursue:

- ISO-9000 is a road map for the implementation of the other four standards.
- ISO-9001 is used by companies to certify their quality systems throughout the product development cycle.
- ISO-9002 is used by companies for whom the focus is on production and installation, often used by companies whose products are already on the market.
- ISO-9003 is used for companies in which comprehensive quality systems may not be important or necessary, such as commodity suppliers.
- ISO-9004 describes recommended quality actions in *should* language, and goes above and beyond the *shall* requirements in the other levels.

Eight Elements of the Excellent Company

1. **A bias for action**, for getting on with it.
2. **Close to the customer**; focused on quality, service, and reliability.
3. **Autonomy and entrepreneurship** within the ranks.
4. **Productivity through people**, instead of through capital improvement or other ways.
5. **Hands-on, value-driven**, with that commitment demonstrated through management actions.
6. **Stick to the knitting**, or focus on businesses you know.
7. **Simple form, lean staff**, especially at top levels. (No company in the study was formally run with a matrix organization structure.)
8. **Simultaneous loose-tight properties**, keeping core values under tight focus and pushing autonomy and empowerment to lower levels of the organization.

Source: Peters and Waterman Jr. 1982, 13–16

Other ISO standards exist for different industries and quality areas, though the 9000 series is most common.

Organizations pursue ISO-900x certification for a number of reasons, often because the standard is particularly common in the European Community nations, and it can aid in competitiveness.

The process of gaining ISO-9000 certification is to work with a third party, called a registrar, who evaluates the quality systems. (Accreditors approve and certify registrars.)

ISO-9000 certification has a reputation for being difficult and time consuming. ISO-9000 expert Greg Hutchins observes:

> If you already have a quality initiative in place, and it has been working properly for a number of years, registration may take as little as six months to a year once the auditors have started. If a company doesn't have a quality program or instead has a cosmetic program—one where quality posters, messages and process control charts are used to convince auditors and customers of a quality commitment—then registration may take two years or more (1993, 12).

To achieve registration, a company must have both a working quality program that complies with the written standards, along with the documentation and control systems to prove compliance, which is the source of the additional work required.

Besides the ISO-900x certification, other systems for auditing and certifying quality exist, including Ford's Q101, GM's Targets of Excellence, or the U.S. military's MIL-Q 9858A. Which one(s)—if any—your organization should pursue depends on your customers and your expansion plans.

Kaizen

One of the motivating forces in the drive for quality improvement is the Japanese challenge that began in the late 1970s. It's well known that some of the underlying tenets of quality management were taught to the Japanese by American experts, including Deming and J. M. Juran. Of course, the Japanese contributed an enormous amount to the development of these concepts, through such leaders as Kaoru Ishikawa (creator of the fishbone diagram) and Taiichi Ohno (creator of kanban, known in the U.S. as *just-in-time* inventory management). It's often observed that certain aspects of Japanese quality programs are reflected in Japanese culture and values, and the argument arises whether those same programs will work in the Western world without modification and rethinking.

Kaizen, Japanese for *ongoing improvement*, is the word most often used in Japan to describe its management methods and techniques. It is a common word, applied to a variety of relationships and situations, and is at the core of process-oriented, rather than results-oriented, thinking (Imai 1986, xxix).

In practice, Kaizen should be considered a subgroup or specific implementation of TQM, focusing on the implementation of Japanese practices directly or with minor modifications into the organizational environment.

Learning Organizations (Senge)

With the rate of change increasing, new initiatives coming along every year or two, the competitive landscape mutating, and technology transforming everything (2), how does an organization cope?

Peter Senge created the model of the learning organization (1990) to address some of the most important problems that result from this level of change. To develop a learning organization, you focus on the *learning disciplines*—lifelong programs of study and practice—as featured in the sidebar.

Management by Exception

Management by exception (MBE) is part of the way to achieve management-by-objectives (MBO) results. If managers are not careful, they bog down in detail, which not only robs you of your time, but also robs your team members of empowerment, autonomy, and personal growth. To apply MBE, you and the team or team member agree in advance on the limits of authority. Everything outside those limits is considered an exception, and exceptions are to be brought to you as a manager. (Exceptions can be higher, lower, or simply different.) Within the grant of authority, teams and team members use their own judgment and are held accountable for agreed-upon performance standards.

MBE promotes empowerment and management development by having work handled at as low a level as possible, and allows focus and effort to be put where the payoff is greatest.

Norma Carr-Ruffino points out that the major disadvantage of MBE is the tendency to focus on the negative—because so many of the exceptions brought to you are at least to some extent admissions of failure. This may create a tendency to hide or at least shade unpleasant realities. Compensate by identifying areas for inspection and attention, and by ensuring positive recognition for proactively bringing problems to you (Carr-Ruffino 1993, 452–53).

The Five Disciplines

1. **Personal Mastery**—expanding our personal capacity to create results and creating an organizational climate to encourage all members to develop themselves.
2. **Mental Models**—reflecting on, clarifying, and improving our internal pictures of the world and seeing how they shape our actions and decisions.
3. **Shared Vision**—building group commitment by developing shared images of the future, with the principles and guiding practices by which we hope to get there.
4. **Team Learning**—transforming conversational and collective thinking skills so that groups can develop intelligence and ability greater than the sum of individual member talents.
5. **Systems Thinking**—thinking about, describing, and understanding the forces and interrelationships that shape the behavior of systems.

Source: Senge, et al. 1994, 6

Management by Objectives

In MBO, the organization begins by establishing a mission statement, which answers these questions: What is our business? Who is the customer? What is value to the customer? What will our business be? What should our business be (Drucker 1973, Chapter 7)? It's vital that mission statements fit certain criteria (Kotler 1984, 45–49):

- It should not claim everything. ("We will be the leading company producing the best products at the lowest price.")
- It should specify the business domain in which the organization will operate.
- It should be motivating, because employees need to feel that their work is significant.
- It should stress major policies that the company plans to honor (valuing teamwork; putting customers first).

The mission statement is turned into specific objectives for each level of management, and that is what is known as MBO. Objectives can be in the areas of profitability, sales growth, market share, innovation, and other areas. Objectives must be realistic, quantified, hierarchical (most to least important), and consistent. These objectives can then be turned into specific action lists and measurement criteria for departments, teams, and individuals (Kotler 1984, 49). The MBO plan is evaluated through benchmarks, which can lead to corrective actions and changes in the plan.

The most common criticism of MBO is that it focuses too tightly on the numbers. Dr. Deming suggests that this leads to "management by fear," with two damaging effects: 1) it encourages short-term performance at the expense of long-term planning (meeting the quarterly MBO goals) with effects in morale and lowered risk-taking, and 2) it increases reliance on those things that can be measured and ignores those things that cannot—including quality (Walton 1986, 90–91). As with many management systems, these defects can be overcome with the right sort of management focus.

Management by Wandering/Walking Around

Such elements as *open-door* policies (first created by IBM's Thomas Watson), the Disney requirement that everyone from the president on down wears a name tag with only his first name on it, and getting management out of the office (named MBWA by Ed Carlson at United Airlines) are all part of an organizational commitment to informal communication, which Peters and Waterman believe is a key component of "organizational fluidity" and supports their model for excellent companies (1982, 121–22).

This relates to a core concept of management as a catalyst within an organization. Catalysts make certain reactions happen while remaining unchanged in the process. A lot of the most important potential value that a manager adds to an organization is hard to measure and quantify, but it's still important.

Scientific Management

Frederick Winslow Taylor, who saw management becoming an exact science, and Max Weber, who invented the bureaucratic organization, developed the first of the approaches to standardizing management as a set of tools in the early years of this century. (At the time, like feudalism in its day, that was an improvement in efficiency, a revolutionary change from what went before.)

Taylor developed the time-and-motion study as the first *efficiency expert*. His idea was that you could break a job into a number of discrete segments. By optimizing the segments and assembling them in a correct structure, efficiency would result—minimize complexity to maximize efficiency.

Taylor is criticized for ignoring the human dimension of workers, treating them as just another piece of equipment. Mary Walton points out, however, that scientific management evolved during a period of mass immigration, when the workplace was being flooded with unskilled and uneducated workers, and it was a period rife with labor strife. By taking discretion away from workers and supervisors through detailed rules and methods for all situations, Taylor believed his system would reduce conflict and eliminate arbitrary uses of power by supervisors (Walton 1986, 9). Theory X management owes a debt to Taylor, and although his ideas today are not widely shared, you only have to look at the way that many organizations actually behave to see Taylor's ideas alive and well in practice.

Self-Directed Work Teams and Other Teams

Virtually every modern management initiative promotes the value of teams, almost to the point of sounding like a panacea. Properly understood, however, teams and teamwork are the necessary foundation to make virtually any of these concepts work. Productivity expert Jim Temme defines teams this way: "A group of people who have been empowered to set goals, make decisions, and solve problems, and who have the commitment to make changes to implement their goals and decisions" (1996, 2).

What distinguishes a team from just another workgroup or division is the two concepts of empowerment and goals. Temme observes (1996, 2):

> *Empowerment* is simply the sharing of power. This means a team must not only be given responsibility for outcomes, but also must have the authority to produce those outcomes.

> *Goals* are absolutely essential to a team's success. In fact, a team is not really a team if it has no goals.

Developing and building teams will become an increasing part of your responsibility in the modern organization. However, different environments and situations produce different kinds of teams, including:

- Quality Circles: Part of the initial focus on Japanese quality involved work teams involved in making suggestions and recommendations for improved quality. These aren't common anymore, because they often had a lack of authority.
- Continuous Improvement Teams (CITs): Part of many TQM efforts. A CIT is formed to improve a particular process, product, or service. It conducts a study, usually using the plan, do, study, act (PDSA) cycle, makes recommendations, and may carry out those recommendations. When the improvement is accomplished, the team goes out of business, or starts on a new problem.
- Project Teams: Similar to CITs, but focused around a project of any sort, whether or not improvement related. Project teams are also often temporary in nature.
- Work Teams: Teams organized around functions, often with cross-training and greater participation in systems and process work. The goal of a work team is to become a …
- Self-Directed Work Team (SDWT). An SDWT is a work team that has reached a level of maturity to enable it to work independently without a supervisor in the conventional sense. SDWTs are self-managed groups.

Statistical Process Control/Statistical Quality Control

Walter A. Shewhart pioneered the use of statistics to improve quality in 1924 when he turned in a one-page memo to the head of AT&T's quality assurance department that included a drawing of what may have been the very first control chart. Shewhart proposed a method for using statistics to improve quality in telephone manufacturing for Western Electric (Dobyns and Crawford-Mason 1991, 52).

Shewhart's insight was to define the limits of random variation in a given worker's task, and determining acceptable highs and lows for the variation, based on statistical analysis. By charting the actual output, any points outside those limits could be detected and the causes studied. Arguably the most important element of Shewhart's "statistical control" was that the workers could be trained to do the charting themselves and therefore make adjustments on their own. This was an early example of empowerment (Walton 1986, 7).

The control chart allows workers to distinguish between variation from common causes and variation from special causes. When special causes are identified, they can be eliminated or reduced, reducing the amount of variation in a process, which leads to improved quality.

From the control chart beginnings, statistical process control (SPC) has acquired a robust set of tools. Deming calls this new set of tools "statistical quality control," and Kaizen calls the tools "quality control" or simply Kaizen. By whatever name, Deming writes:

> Education in simple but powerful statistical technique is required of all people in management, all engineers and scientists, inspectors, quality control managers, management in the service organizations of the company, such as accounting, payroll, purchase, safety, legal department, consumer service, consumer research. … Five days under a competent teacher will suffice as a base (Walton 1986, 97).

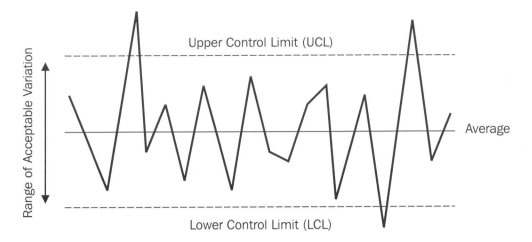

Figure 7   SPC Control Chart

There are additional tools, but these are most common. You'll find these statistical tools have wide application in problem solving and process improvement, regardless of whether your organization is involved in the quality movement. It's a good idea to become familiar with them and their use (3).

Total Quality Management

A lot of the current emphasis on management practices, theories, and systems can ultimately be traced to the Japanese challenge, which forced American business to rethink traditional methods.

There are several schools of thought in TQM, and if your organization uses or plans to use TQM, then it's important for you to know what type of TQM is to be used.

Regardless of the specific approach or guru used by your organization, the basic TQM philosophy is based on three interlinking goals: continuous improvement, customer focus, and teamwork.

Continuous improvement is the essence of the work of TQM. The systems, processes, and methods of the organization are there to get the work accomplished. Systems produce what they are designed to produce—if they are designed to produce poor quality, they do. To improve quality in any meaningful manner, you must look at the way that the work is performed and look for improvements. Improvements may be small or large—even the small ones add up. This is a never-ending process, because improvement is always possible. Continuous improvement is usually accomplished by teams, and the teams normally follow some version of the Shewhart Cycle (sometimes called the Deming Cycle): PDSA. (This used to be plan, do, check, act, or PDCA, but Deming considered *study* a better word.)

Customer focus refers to the purpose of quality. While quality for its own sake is a nice concept, the business reality is that quality must help achieve the organizational mission. Earlier, you learned the TQM definition of quality: "What the customer wants, their overriding focus, is to have their *expectations* met (and exceeded if possible)" [Berkowitz 1994, 6]. In other words, the definition of quality must be based on customer needs, wants, and expectations. If it doesn't meet the needs, wants, or expectations of the customer, then it's hard to

---

The Seven Basic Tools of SPC

1. **Cause and Effect Diagram**. Also known as the fishbone diagram or the Ishikawa diagram, this tool is used in brainstorming sessions to identify the potential cause or causes of a given effect or outcome.
2. **Flow Chart**. To improve a process, it's first necessary to study it. Do a flow chart of the way it works now, looking for ways to improve the process.
3. **Pareto Chart**. Based on the Pareto Principle, this chart involves tabulating and graphing the different causes for a given problem so that you can sort out the "vital few" (major causes) from the "trivial many" (minor causes).
4. **Run Chart**. The run chart is like a control chart without the upper and lower control limits defined. It is uscd to look for trends over time.
5. **Histogram**. The histogram is a standard statistical tool that graphs frequency distribution in a bar form.
6. **Scatter Diagram**. Charts possible relationships between changes observed in two different sets of variables.
7. **Control Chart**. The original tool is still part of the process.

---

argue how relevant it is. One problem in quality movements is that certain technical professionals admire elegant engineering or software code for its own sake, rather than for the benefit to the customer. This is not quality.

Teams refers to the approach that the organization takes to achieve progress in the other two legs of the triangle. Teaming expert Temme observes:

> For continuous improvement to have an impact rather than just be a rallying cry, there must be input for improvement from all levels in the organization. Many of the companies that have successfully implemented TQM have consequently formed work teams to solve customer problems, to improve products and services, to make decisions on how to proceed, and continuously train team members. Total quality management and team building, therefore, go hand in hand (1996, 4).

Who's Who in Total Quality Management

The three main Western approaches to TQM are based on the works, respectively, of Deming, Juran, and Philip Crosby. (Other quality experts also have their adherents, but these three are the best known.) While with most approaches the proponents emphasize thc differences, the similarities in approaches actually outweigh those differences.

Deming

According to Lloyd Dobyns, "Deming is the philosopher; the others are more pragmatic. ... People who believe in his method have been known to compare it to religion, because, they say, it not only improves quality in manufacturing, service, government, and education, but it

Figure 8 The Three Foundations of TQM

also makes their lives better" (Dobyns and Crawford-Mason 1991, 56). The Deming method revolves around fourteen points (see sidebar), which provide a philosophical foundation for effective quality management.

Juran

He actually worked with Shewhart at AT&T's Hawthorne Plant. (Deming worked there as well, but in R&D and didn't meet Shewhart until later.) While Deming sees managing for quality as requiring transformation, Juran believes that it is more analogous to managing for finance. The Juran Trilogy® of quality planning, quality control, and quality improvement is at the core of his method. Less statistics oriented than Deming, Juran focuses on senior management behavior, believing that by putting as much emphasis on quality as most do on finance, senior management can lead the necessary steps (Dobyns and Crawford-Mason 1991, 69–71).

Crosby

He has two distinctions: he's the only one of the major quality gurus without a doctorate, and he's the only one who directly managed operations programs. He left ITT as corporate vice president for quality to publish his best-selling book, *Quality Is Free*, and to consult. If your program involves the concept of zero defects, you're working with a Crosby model. His *Absolutes of Quality Management* are listed in the sidebar.

Again, remember that these programs have more similarities than differences. You can benefit by studying all of them, although you will need to put your emphasis where the organization places its.

Workforce 2000

Three key trends were first identified in a highly influential and controversial study known as Workforce 2000 (Kutchner 1988, 1–7): first, that the share of the workforce held by women, minorities, and immigrants would grow much faster than white males; second, that there would be a growing shortage of skilled workers because of inequalities in education; and third, the "birth dearth" (post-baby boom) generation cohort would lower availability of younger workers, causing further changes in the structure of the workforce.

The implications for business and management are significant. First, it emphasizes the need for increased commitment to training and staff development. Second, it is the primary

Deming's Fourteen Points

1. Create constancy of purpose for improvement of product and service.
2. Adopt the new philosophy.
3. Cease dependence on mass inspection.
4. End the practice of awarding business on price tag alone.
5. Improve constantly and forever the system of production and service.
6. Institute training.
7. Institute leadership.
8. Drive out fear.
9. Break down barriers between staff areas.
10. Eliminate slogans, exhortations, and targets for the workforce.
11. Eliminate numerical quotas.
12. Remove barriers to pride of workmanship.
13. Institute a vigorous program of education and retraining.
14. Take action to accomplish the transformation.

Source: Walton 1986, 34–36; 55–88 (discussion)

Crosby's Absolutes of Quality Management

Quality means conformance to requirements, not elegance.

There is no such thing as a quality problem.

There is no such thing as the economics of quality; it is always cheaper to do the job right the first time.

The only performance measurement is the cost of quality.

The only performance standard is zero defects.

Source: Crosby 1980, 111–12

source of the emphasis for workplace programs on cultural diversity, the process of improving communications, understanding, and acceptance among people with different cultural outlooks, because the *white male* homogenous workforce will no longer be a norm.

The controversy surrounding Workforce 2000 has to do with the validity of the statistical trend analysis. Critics suggest that those trends have been exaggerated. Worse, a typographical error in the executive summary caused an overreaction to the report: instead of correctly reporting that only 15 percent of net additions to the workforce would be white males, the word *net* was omitted, suggesting that only 15 percent of all workforce entrants would be white males (Crittenden 1994, 18).

Regardless of the trend analysis, however, it's certainly the fact that the composition of the workforce, technical and nontechnical alike, will change with regard to sex and ethnicity in the years to come. Whether the change is fast or slow, dramatic or gradual, it's important for you to meet your responsibilities in working with diverse groups and individuals.

Zero-Base Budgeting

Zero-base budgeting (ZBB) was a major fad in the late 1970s. The Carter Administration mandated use of ZBB in all federal agencies. Historically, the baseline for next year's budget was always this year's budget, and amounts were adjusted up (and occasionally even down) based on the previous year's figures. Using the ZBB approach, the baseline for next year's budget is always set at zero. In other words, each department, program, or activity must rejustify its very existence rather than have it taken for granted, and build its budget request from the ground up.

Like BPR, in which "obliterate, don't automate" takes you back to a ground-zero rethinking approach, ZBB is designed to keep programs and activities focused on core business objectives and the bottom line.

What Makes These Methods Successful (or Not)

One important difference between management systems and technical systems is that attitudes and commitment have a lot to do with eventual success. Skepticism in the workforce concerning these new management initiatives is not so much skepticism about the theory as it is about the drive and commitment—and sometimes intelligence—of the managers and executives leading the charge.

The question—and the answer is obvious—is: How seriously will the workforce in this organization (see Case Study 11) take any new management initiative? This situation is not the fault of MBWA as a theory and concept, but rather the fault of the individual implementation. Much of the criticism leveled at these initiatives comes back to the question of how they are implemented in practice.

Be careful not to confuse the concept of *less than perfect* with the concept of *utterly worthless and a big waste of time*, a problem you'll encounter in trying to communicate with certain technical professionals. Engineers know that no mechanical process can be 100 percent efficient; waste is inevitable in any transfer of energy. Why, then, should anyone expect management to violate the Second Law of Thermodynamics? A certain amount of waste and friction is guaranteed no matter how successful the management initiative turns out to be; accepting the reality and learning to look for the positives is very important.

Be Patient

Be careful not to expect too much too fast. Physical objects have inertia—the tendency of a body at rest to stay at rest, the tendency of a body once in motion to remain in motion until acted upon by an outside force. People and organizations have effective inertia, and change will always be harder and slower than you expect. To change the momentum of an object, you

---

Case Study 11

People Unclear on the Concept II

The CEO of a $30 million corporation decided to practice MBWA. This was announced in a memorandum to the workforce, along with schedules to inform each department when the CEO would *wander around*. Employees were told to be prepared and ready for these visits.

Each department cleaned and straightened for the *wandering* visits. The department head escorted the CEO around to selected cubicles for *chats*. Workers were briefed in advance what to say, how to address the CEO, and what subjects to avoid.

The initiative lasted two weeks. The CEO felt that it took too much time away from important executive responsibilities.

---

can either apply a large amount of force over a short period of time, or a smaller amount of force over a long period of time. The second option is more likely the only one available to you, and even to senior management.

Be careful to avoid *career-limiting moves*, which are self-defeating organizational behaviors, such as explaining to the CEO exactly why she is wrong on the issues.

> "Maybe they think they're ... expendable," [Fowler said].
>
> "Wrong," said Renner.
>
> "The tactful way," Rod said quietly, "the polite way to disagree with the Senator would be to say, 'That turns out not to be the case'" (Niven and Pournelle 1974, 417).

Just Do It

Finally, be proactive. Once there has been a leadership decision to start a new management initiative, it's incumbent (and politically savvy) on you to find out what the initiative is, its sources, and how and when it will be implemented. Go to the library or bookstore, and get the written material. Read it yourself. Take the time to discover any contrary points of view or problem histories. Volunteer to take a leadership role in the implementation of the initiative, whatever it is, and *walk the talk* yourself, regardless of how well you think others are doing it. Train the members of your team in it, and help them to see the positive potential both organizationally and personally. (There is almost always some, even though most people will fear reorganization and downsizing.) You will not only improve the chances of success of the initiative, but you'll also gain credibility and support at higher levels of the organization and even with your own staff.

Exercise 13

Preparing for Management Fads and Initiatives

Whether your organization is already at work on a management initiative, or whether it is getting ready to announce one, you need to be prepared by answering the following questions.

1. What is the name of the management initiative?

   _____

   _____

   _____

2. Which senior managers or executives are the champions of the initiative?

   _____

   _____

   _____

3. Which books, seminars, tapes, or videos have they used in their learning, and which experts are they using as models? (You need to study the same resources.)

   _____

   _____

   _____

4. What has been the organization's previous experience with management initiatives, both positive and negative?

   _____

   _____

   _____

5. What barriers do you see for the new initiative, and how might they be overcome (organizational structure, some executives fighting it, worker fears and concerns, previous track record, and so on)?

   _____

   _____

   _____

6. What factors do you see supporting the new initiative, and how can they be enhanced (real commitment, good practices, previous track record, and so on)?

   _____

   _____

   _____

7. How will the success or failure of the program affect you personally? Your team members?

_____

_____

_____

8. What steps can you take to maximize payoff for yourself and your team? (This isn't merely selfish; it's part of building meaningful commitment.)

_____

_____

_____

9. What steps can you take to make it work for the organization and its customers and stakeholders?

_____

_____

_____

10. How can you demonstrate your support for the new program?

_____

_____

_____

Debrief of Exercise 13

Good planning and good analysis help make any plan more successful. Because of the potential impact, it's vital that you be proactive in any management initiative—the alternative can be devastating. Remember that the ultimate success of the management initiative depends on many variables: commitment from the top, effective planning, and support from the intervening levels of management—and that includes you.

Notes

1. The converse tends to be true as well. Almost any idea, implemented by thoughtless and uncommitted management, is certainly doomed to fail.
2. "Any sufficiently advanced technology is indistinguishable from magic" (Clarke 1999, 413). "Any technology indistinguishable from magic is insufficiently advanced" (Benford 1997).
3. An excellent reference is Brassard and Ritter 1994.

Section Three
MANAGING TECHNICAL PROFESSIONALS

Managing technical professionals involves a number of interrelated disciplines. The first, of course, is a solidly prepared and self-aware manager, which was the focus of the first section. Second is command of the fundamental skills of management and supervision, which was the focus of the second section.

Technical professionals are, of course, people first (though some may give you cause to doubt it). The first set of skills to try comprises the regular skills of staff management. However, there are unique, or at least unusual, elements in this situation, and you need to develop a third set of skills, which is the focus of this section.

The first element of this skill set is to understand and manage aspects of corporate or departmental culture, the overall influencer and shaper of technical behavior.

The second element involves mastering methods of team structure and work organization, the process of shaping the accomplishment of work. Should you have a team focus, or should you plan for people to work independently?

The third element involves technical professionals as individuals: how to manage them, how to deal with problems and power conflicts, and even how to manage someone with greater technical knowledge than you possess in certain areas.

Finally, your challenge is to extend your reach and influence throughout the organization, to work effectively with managers, other departments, customers, and others on whom you depend but over whom you have limited control.

Chapter 9
TechnoCulture

Understanding Corporate Culture

The anthropological concept of *culture* involves certain norms that develop within a group that is thrown together over time. Culture develops primarily as a result of proximity, and secondarily as a result of common interests, styles, and goals. While not everyone within a culture subscribes to all its dictates—and some even reject the culture in which they find themselves—the culture nevertheless influences each member.

The concept of *corporate culture* is very important in analyzing organizational dynamics, and many organizations seeking to accomplish major change try to change the corporate culture itself. The *vision statement* is often a statement of the nature of the culture that the organization would like to have, listing such characteristics as teamwork, common goal sharing, free communication up and down, integrity, customer focus, and so on.

It's equally valid and important, therefore, to take a look at the concept of a technical professional culture. In high-tech organizations such as Microsoft or Hewlett-Packard, the technical professional culture may be the organizational culture.

In other organizations, the technical functions are not the center of the organization. They may be staff departments, such as information technology. They may be line departments, such as a product development group at a marketing-driven company such as Proctor and Gamble. In those organizations, there may be long-standing conflict between the technical departments and everybody else.

As a manager of technical professionals, you need to 1) analyze the culture of your group, 2) determine how it fits (or doesn't fit) with the culture of the overall organization, 3) learn how to modify problems or difficulties in the technical culture, so that it accomplishes the work and has satisfactory relationships throughout the organization, and 4) develop the culture of your department or team in light of organizational change, mission, vision, and values.

The most important thing to keep in mind as you do this work is that change takes time. Even if you do everything perfectly, expect a significant lag between your efforts and accomplishment of the desired changes. Look for help, build support, and accept the reality of imperfection in the process.

Glossary of TechnoCulture Terms

404: Clueless (from the error message given by a Web browser when it can't find the requested site).

Adminisphere: Those in charge of the organization, whose offices have actual walls.

Appeasement Engineer: A computer repair technician whose job is to arrive at the site, make sure that the machine is plugged in, then call the home office for further instructions.

Betamaxed: Being left behind by new technology breakthroughs.

Bit Diddlers: People who produce, write, or sell computer code or bits.

Chainsaw Consultants: People called in by the adminisphere to increase efficiency by use of layoffs.

Chip Jewelry: Outdated computer equipment.

Circling the Drain: Waiting for the ax to fall.

Code Pie: Pizza, the favorite food of programmers.

Cube Farm: Where each worker is assigned to her own cubicle.

Dawn Patrol: All-night work sessions fueled by java, Jolt, and code pie, and motivated by fear of chainsaw consultants and being betamaxed.

Digerati: The *digital literati*, or people sophisticated about new cybertechnology.

Encrypted English: Poor writing skills.

Geekosphere: The personalized area around each cubicle, filled with monitor pets.

Geeksploitation: The skill of those in the adminisphere to get Bit Diddlers to work the dawn patrol.

Java: Coffee. ("Coffee comes in five descending stages: Coffee, Java, Jamoke, Joe, and Carbon Remover. This stuff was no better than grade four" [Heinlein 1963, 74].

Jitterati: The tendency of the Digerati to work in horribly competitive work environments with frequent jolts of coffee, universally called Java.

Jolt: High caffeine/real-sugar cola beverage.

Monitor Pets: Toys, family pictures, and old convention badges, often stuck on the computer monitor.

PEBCAK: "Problem exists between chair and keyboard": Appeasement Engineer term for user-created problem.

Treeware: Paper computer manuals.

WAW: Waiter-Actor-Webmaster.

Source: Branwyn 1997, Section 5, Page 5

Characteristics of Technical Cultures

In the movie *Big*, in which Tom Hanks magically turns from a fourteen-year-old boy into a grownup and goes to work for a toy company, his first job with the company is as an order-entry clerk. Excited and highly motivated, he's working very quickly when the person in the next cubicle, played by Jon Lovitz, leans over the cube wall and hisses, "What do you think you're doing?"

Shocked, Hanks replies that he's trying to do his job—is he doing it wrong? But that's not Lovitz' concern. "Slow down," he says, "You're going to make the rest of us look bad!" And Hanks does, proving that corporate culture isn't exclusively the province of executive management. The corporate, department, or even team culture is highly influenced by the attitudes and behaviors of the members of the community at all levels. Peer pressure is alive and well. While individuals in the corporate culture may react against the dominant behaviors and attitudes, they are still influenced by them.

The first step in working with your technoculture is to analyze it, and that's the goal of the next exercise.

Exercise 14

Culture Characteristics

Turn back to Exercise 1. Instead of answering the questions for yourself, answer them for the members of your team. For example, the first question reads:

Characteristic	STRONGLY DESCRIBES		SOMEWHAT DESCRIBES		NOT AT ALL
1. Values logic over emotions	5	4	3	2	1

Consider the overall tendency of your team rather than the attitudes of given participants. You might think about behavior at staff meetings, reactions to new ideas, ways in which peer pressure *puts down* nonconformists, and so on. Would you say that the team culture is pure Mr. Spock, or Dr. Spock instead?

Continue this for all the questions in the exercise. Then list the following:

1. Positive characteristics of work culture (those that aid productivity):

   _____
   _____
   _____
   _____

2. Negative characteristics of work culture (those that inhibit productivity):

_____
_____
_____
_____

3. Elements of technical arrogance or self-centeredness (those that cause internal and external customers to be invalidated):

_____
_____
_____
_____

4. Elements of focus on quality and improvement (use of Total Quality Management [TQM] and other tools):

_____
_____
_____
_____
_____

5. Level of energy and drive (ways in which the team supports or drains energy from coworkers):

_____
_____
_____
_____

6. Relationships with other departments and organization as a whole:

_____
_____
_____
_____

7. Degree of organizational fit (how your team culture fits in with the rest of the organization's culture):

_____
_____
_____
_____

Debrief of Exercise 14

In this exercise, you have conducted an analysis of your group culture and determined how well it fits (or doesn't fit) with the culture of the overall organization.

You may have come up with some of the same observations as other technical managers:

■ The members of my team are perceived by the organization as unnecessarily obscure and technology oriented, rather than focused on customer needs.

- My team members perceive the rest of the organization as helpless and incompetent, and definitely not as bright as they are.
- You can always tell a member of my team by his dress—our members stand out in some unfortunate ways.
- The members of my team are highly competitive with each other about technical skill, and end up doing things the hard way just to show off.

You should have identified both strengths and weaknesses in your team culture. Strengths can be in terms of commitment to the work, to quality, and to technical achievement and excellence, as long as that doesn't lead to noncustomer-focused work. What can you do about the weaknesses?

Overcoming Change Resistance

"One should bear in mind," says Niccoló Machiavelli, "that there is nothing as difficult to handle, more dubious in outcome, or more dangerous to organise, than the assumption of responsibility for the introduction of a new form of government" (1908, 55). Change resistance—especially involving changes in management practices and goals—is one of the fundamental realities with which you must deal. Yet change is essential in the modern organization.

Organizational and team cultures are a key element of current study. Some organizational cultures are diseased and need major surgery. Others are fundamentally sound, but are still capable of improvement and growth. Changing organizational culture is always a challenge area, but it can be done.

Remember the earlier discussion of inertia as it applies to people and organizations? The larger the team, the longer it has been in existence, and the more people are set in their ways, the greater the inertia with which you must deal. You will most likely be in a position in which change will result from the steady application of moderate force over significant time, although sometimes you discover that you can create greater change than you think.

The organizational change model in Figure 9 tells us that the difficulty involved in changing someone's knowledge is lower than changing an attitude, which in turn is lower than changing individual behavior, and finally lower than changing group behavior. The same is true for the amount of time involved. You can easily and pretty quickly convince someone that smoking is bad for one's health, but that person may still have a poor attitude about quitting smoking: "So it'll kill me in twenty years. So what?" Changing the attitude is harder. Persuading someone to actually give up smoking is harder yet, and making an entire workforce quit smoking in order to reduce health insurance outlays, harder yet.

The Power of *Top-Down* Change

The conventional attack is to start at the bottom of the chart and work your way up, providing knowledge, working to change attitudes, and so forth, in turn. What is not as intuitive is that *top-down* change is often more effective—in other words, enforcing a change in organizational (group) behavior and letting the change filter down to the level of knowledge. The military uses top-down change in basic training—for example, by making new recruits drill immediately—with the knowledge that attitudes and eventually understanding will follow, and in most cases it does. Parents use top-down change with young children; it's not necessary that the two-year-old know that playing in the street is dangerous or even to have a good attitude about not playing in the street—those things will come in time, and obviously much more effectively if the child is still alive.

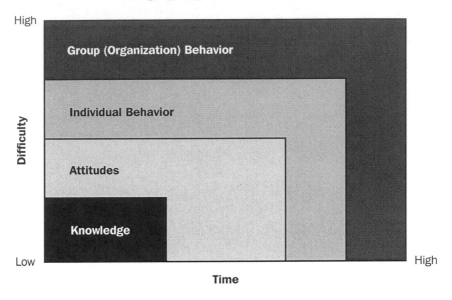

Figure 9 Organizational Change Model

Especially if you have just entered a position, or there has been a major organizational change, you may find it quite useful to adopt a top-down approach. The difficulty is, of course, that you have to show strength and consistency during the transition, because you are likely to encounter a great deal of resistance. The advantage is that the top-down process often takes less time and results in better implementation of the change.

Modifying Organizational Culture

Given that change is difficult and time consuming, use this seven-step model for planning and achieving organizational change:

1. Set goals.
2. Give reasons.
3. Build allies.
4. Be consistent.
5. Be patient.
6. Settle for less than perfect.
7. Do it again.

Set Goals

The fundamental step in changing organizational culture is to determine exactly what change you are seeking by using the SMART (specific, measurable, agreed-upon, realistic, time-specific) goal model. Examples are to become more customer focused, to have better relationships with other departments, to work as a team, to communicate effectively, or to implement new management initiatives (TQM, business process reengineering, and so on). Try to limit the number of goals that you are pursuing at any one time.

How will you measure accomplishment and progress? One of the most powerful tools in getting others to work toward your goals is to give them a behavioral and measurable standard that they must meet. If your goal is to become more customer focused, you could measure that by reduction in complaints, repeat business, fewer defects and do-overs, or how well customers operate the system that you designed for them, for example. If you want people to work as a team, you could measure that by increased productivity, fewer conflicts among team members, amount of cooperation and support given and received, and so on.

Give Reasons

Since a common characteristic of technical professionals is their need to know why, reasons— important for all groups—become critical. Why do you want to be more customer focused, for example? How does that benefit the organization? How does it benefit the team and individuals on the team? Are there costs or negative consequences involved? What are they, and how will they affect team members? Note that "because the suits in executive-land say so" doesn't qualify as an adequate reason for the purpose of changing behavior.

Build Allies

The old joke points out that the world's most popular radio station has the call letters WII-FM, which stands for "What's in it for me?" Everyone listens all the time. You need support among your team members to make change happen.

A common mistake is to rely on the backing of senior management as the source of your authority and power to make changes in subordinates' behaviors. Machiavelli warns against this: "He who becomes prince with the aid of the nobles finds it more difficult to stay in power than he who becomes prince with the aid of the people, for he finds himself surrounded by many who consider themselves his equal, and consequently is unable to govern and manage them as he would wish" (1908, 69).

What are the benefits to team members in achieving the organizational change? To determine this, also be honest about costs. If the department becomes more customer focused, it clearly benefits the customer and may well benefit stockholders and executives; but if the team members believe that they will see no personal benefit for the extra work, why should they care? If they are likely to receive benefits, such as participation in profit sharing, then you can help them see the potential cash payoff from the behavior; but noncash benefits are often more reliable in achieving the desired change. For example, greater customer contact may result in greater influence on decisions and outcomes.

You can achieve change without the support of everyone as long as you have key influencers behind you. It's often the case that one or two members of your team have disproportionate influence over the others. If they turn against you or the change you seek, their power is often great enough to stymie you. Rewards for them—increased influence, relationships, knowledge, and power, for example—may result in increased support from the whole team.

Be Consistent

It's sometimes more important to be consistent than always right, even remembering Ralph Waldo Emerson's warning that "a foolish consistency is the hobgoblin of little minds." Consistency of vision, mission, and values doesn't fall into the "foolish" category. Being inflexible about details, timetables, and implementation can become foolish. The slogan, "walk the talk," has been repeated to death, but it's still a valuable concept.

If you want the department to be more customer focused, you must be customer focused yourself. You must support and praise steps that team members take that are more customer focused than before; you must not reward or make exceptions for shortcuts that don't meet customer needs and expectations; you must evaluate people on their support and efforts toward the goal; and you must keep this behavior up over time.

The corollary is, of course, that it's unwise to set goals for organizational change that you can't personally get excited about.

Be Patient

While you may in some cases have the power to achieve change through great force in small periods of time, far more often you must work to achieve change by consistent smaller force over much longer periods of time. Reinforce the idea of progress in yourself and in others, and accept the likely reality that it will take much longer than you plan. "Genius," observed George Louis Leclerc de Buffon on his admission to the French Academy in 1753, "is nothing but a great aptitude for patience."

Settle for Less than Perfect

No machine operates with 100 percent efficiency, nor can you expect any change involving people or organizations to achieve 100 percent efficiency. Understanding the value and realism of *less than perfect but good enough* is helpful for your sanity as well as for long-term effectiveness. As science fiction author Robert Heinlein wrote:

> "But being rational … " [said the Professor], "he tries to live perfectly in an imperfect world … aware that his efforts will be less than perfect yet undismayed by self-knowledge of self-failure."
>
> "Hear, hear!" I said. "'Less than perfect.' What I've been aiming for all my life."
>
> "You've achieved it," said Wyoh (1968, 64).

The key to working with *less than perfect* is to identify *good enough*. What is the level of change that would be considered satisfactory, and how would you measure it? How will you determine whether progress is taking place, and how can you celebrate that progress?

Please note that this is not intended as an excuse for failure to strive. Heinlein's professor does try to live perfectly, but knows that the goal will never be realized. Constant striving produces regular movement, and you can always trust movement.

Do It Again

The contemporary organizational model is one of constant change and transformation. One benefit of working for change in organizational culture is that you can condition people to work more effectively in the environment of continual change. Tom Peters observes, "The most important and visible outcropping of the [bias for action] of the excellent companies is their willingness to try things out, to experiment" (Peters and Waterman Jr. 1982, 134).

Two important elements to consider are: 1) as you see movement on one element of improvement, start another element, using the same model, and 2) don't be afraid to experiment. Certain changes will fail, and that's not a problem. Peters notes, "Experimentation acts as a form of cheap learning for most of the excellent companies, usually proving less costly— and more useful—than sophisticated market research or careful staff planning" (Peters and Waterman Jr. 1982, 143).

Chapter 10
Teams and Structure

Organizational and Team Structures—Which Is Best for You?

Another of the key strategic decisions that you must make as a manager of technical professionals has to do with the internal structure: to team or not to team; that is the question.

The right answer, as in so many cases, is situational: the nature of the work, the organization, and the goals to be achieved come together to help decide on proper structure. The questions shown in Figure 10 will help you make the right decision about group structure.

Project or Work?

The first question to consider is whether the activities and goals of your department, team, or workgroup are project oriented or work oriented.

Project versus Work

Project	Work
Goal oriented: Has a beginning, a middle, and an end.	Ongoing: There is no defined point at which the work is planned to be over.
Consists of tasks that can be put into a connected and interrelated sequence.	Tasks may or may not be able to be put into a connected and interrelated sequence.
Has a limited duration.	Is ongoing.
Unique and nonroutine.	A primary, repetitive element of your job.

Source: Dobson 1996, 4–5

You'll often find that certain elements fit the project model and other elements fit the work model. The important question to consider is which dominates your time. If the major activities of your job are all in the project category, and the work elements are secondary, then you should organize your team on a project model. If not, then you should organize on a work model.

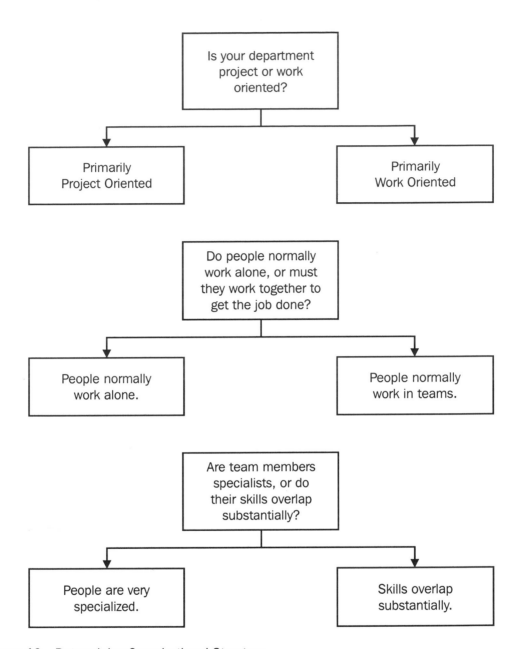

Figure 10 Determining Organizational Structure

Solo or Group?

The second consideration is whether the work or projects in your area is or are primarily done by solo professionals, or whether people must work in teams to get the work accomplished. In software development, for example, you might have a situation in which individual service needs come from internal customers, and one person is assigned responsibility for developing, testing, and implementing the necessary code. In the very same business, however, you might find that the work being requested is large enough that you need to establish a team of programmers to develop it.

You may be in a level of management in which your department or workgroup exists as a team inside someone else's project, but the members of your group do their work as solo professionals. If so, consider your work to fit the *solo* category.

Your department or team can be project oriented and solo, project oriented and group, work oriented and solo, or work oriented and group.

Specialists or Overlapping Skills?

In a new product development team, you might have programmers, electronics engineers, industrial engineers, graphic designers, copywriters, and marketing specialists working together. There's relatively little skill overlap here, and the skill sets are diverse enough that cross-training is not a very strong option.

If the team is all programmers, but some members are database specialists, others expert in accounting application, and still others networking specialists, the skill sets are diverse; but with a concentration on cross-training, people can become competent in the different functional areas.

If the team is all programmers and any programmer or group of programmers can handle any of the assignments you typically receive, skill overlap is high, and the need for cross-training is minimal.

Armed with your answers to these questions, use Exercise 15 to choose a structure that makes sense for your specific situation.

Exercise 15

Choosing Organizational Structure

Situation	Individual	Specialist Group	Project Team	Self-Directed Work Teams
Project Oriented Solo Specialized	X			
Project Oriented Solo Overlapping Skills	X			X
Project Oriented Team Specialized			X	X
Project Oriented Team Overlapping Skills			X	X
Work Oriented Solo Specialized	X			
Work Oriented Solo Overlapping Skills	X			X
Work Oriented Team Specialized		X		
Work Oriented Team Overlapping Skills		X		X

Debrief of Exercise 15

You now have identified one or more structures for organizing your workgroup, and in the next few pages you'll learn about these concepts.

What if you have more than one structure from which to choose, or what if the nature of your work is that your category changes frequently?

First, the structural concepts are not either/or. You can choose a dominant structure and still vary it, based on projects or work situations.

Second, you can hybridize the types of structures, borrowing elements from different ideas to form a structure that is right for your possibly unique situation.

Third, you can reorganize the workgroup into a new structure when the need arises.

Individual-Oriented Workgroup Structure

When the work is solo in nature, it's natural for people to work as individuals, not as teams. The job of the manager is to parcel the various projects and/or work assignments; the individuals complete those assignments, and the manager oversees to ensure quality and productivity.

If skills are shared, who gets what job assignment depends largely on who's available at a given time, and who has too many current job assignments. If skills are not shared, the subject matter of the assignment determines who gets it, or at least narrows the choices.

While structurally simple, the individual-oriented workgroup structure presents a wide range of management challenges.

Different Skill Levels/Work Maturities

As a manager, you need first to honestly assess the varying skill levels (ability to do the work) and work maturities (self-starting professional behavior) of your team members. Your ability to distribute job assignments and get the work done is strongly affected by those levels.

The two common mistakes that you can make are 1) overloading your top performers in an effort to ensure quality and timely performance, and 2) failing to develop and grow those staff with lower skill levels or work maturity.

The best way to avoid the first problem is to focus on the second problem instead. That means working with the individuals who need development either in their technical skills or in behavioral aspects of their work performance.

Individual development plans. The individual development plan (IDP) is a powerful and effective tool to deal long term with skill and work maturity (1). Basically, an IDP is a negotiated, written document between supervisor and team member, setting forth growth and development goals for a period of time (traditionally a year, but shorter periods may be easier to keep in focus). When IDPs are misused and ineffective, it's often because the manager (and team member) regarded it as a one-way process: "Let me tell you what you need to do to shape up." Instead, an effective IDP requires the manager (and the organization), as well as the team member, to take some steps.

Examples of IDP steps might include: arranging for formal training in deficient areas, providing regular feedback, stating specific behaviors that the team member needs to follow, and so on. An IDP should carry weight in the next performance-appraisal cycle and in consideration for raises and bonuses, both for successfully achieving IDP goals and for failing to do so.

Desirability/Futility of Certain Assignments

In the real world, some job assignments are always better than others. Some lead to organizational visibility, bonuses, and promotions, while others are dead ends or even worse. Some are technically challenging and fun and may even give you trips to great cities, armed with a fat expense account. Some are boring, involve working with difficult and technically ignorant customers, and send you to unpleasant places to stay in cheap roach-infested hotels. It's inevitable that individuals on your team will recognize the difference and will campaign for the best assignments, using a range of tactics from the professional to the actively manipulative. Failure to get the job assignments that they want can lead some team members to sulk, turn in poor performance on other projects, or even resign.

How to Give Out Great Job Assignments

Technique	Advantages	Problems	Success Tips
Give top performers (quality and attitude) the plum assignments.	1) Motivates positive behavior. 2) Rewards best people.	1) People question your definition of *best*. 2) Suspicion of playing favorites and having self-fulfilling prophecies.	1) Make sure that your criteria for excellence are both objective and shared with others. 2) Work to help others develop to the same skill level. 3) Especially in a busy organization, don't make all assignments purely merit based.
Systematically rotate good and bad job assignments among all team members.	1) Fairly objective way to ensure that no one is singled out. 2) Can motivate all team members equally.	1) Doesn't reinforce desirable behavior. 2) *Good* and *bad* can be subjective. 3) May end in arguments about whose turn it is.	1) Keep a written list of assignments to ensure that you don't forget whose turn it is.
Give each job assignment to the next available team member without any consideration for whether it's a goodie or a zonk.	1) Avoids arguments. 2) Focuses on the jobs, not people's personal interests.	1) May be hard to figure whose turn is next, especially if people finish assignments on irregular schedules. 2) Someone may get a run of good or bad assignments, causing jealousy and friction.	1) Only use this when people finish job assignments on clear deadlines. 2) Date stamp incoming jobs and finished jobs to limit opportunity for argument.

You can't please all of the people all of the time. It's important to realize up front that there is no possible way that you can make everyone happy here, no matter how scrupulously professional and fair you try to be. Nevertheless, being scrupulously professional and fair is the best strategy that you can follow.

You have several possible methods for spreading the goodies and the zonks (2), as shown in the sidebar. Valid arguments exist for each of the methods presented in the sidebar. How should you make your choice? Here are some options:

- The nature of the work environment
- Traditions and corporate culture
- Your personal management style
- Your values and the values of your management
- A focus group to let the group decide.

Focus groups. The fifth technique has several advantages: 1) it promotes group empowerment by letting the group make decisions, 2) it takes some of the onus for difficult decisions off your shoulders in a legitimate fashion, 3) it promotes consistency and a sense of fairness, and 4) it reduces (but probably won't eliminate) complaints.

In fact, whatever you pick, be consistent in application, and expect to have people complain or fight about whatever decisions you make.

Overloading

Unbalanced skill sets and widely divergent levels of work maturity can result in overloading of certain people. This is a different problem from that of everyone being overloaded because of the massive total amount of work to be done. When some people are overloaded and others have much less on their plates, a variety of problems sets in, including damage to the morale of the overloaded team members and damage to the self-esteem of those who are at least comparatively underworked.

Staff development. One solution to the problem of overloading is providing staff development to less skilled, less work-mature staff through the IDP process discussed earlier. However, if the problem is that your environment doesn't support cross-training in different skills, this may not solve it.

Process improvement. Another solution involves applying the total quality management/ business process reengineering ideas of process improvement and process reengineering to the work of your department. Why are some people overloaded? What is the nature of the work they are doing and the way they are doing it? Can the way in which the work is being done be speeded up or changed? If so, you can reduce overwork.

Getting more help. A third solution involves careful documentation of workload and skill level so that you can make a strong business case to management for additional team members in the affected area or with the less-available skill set. To get this, you don't just have to demonstrate that overwork exists; you must instead show—with facts and numbers—that the additional person will result in additional profit or net lower costs to the organization. This is sometimes difficult to do, but it is possible.

Deadline Management

With each member of your team working on his individual project or work assignment—especially if the specific assignments are comparatively small and the number of assignments is comparatively large—you have the technical challenge of keeping track of assignment status, identifying those heading for trouble and lateness, and ensuring that deadlines are met.

Tracking multiple projects. In a multiple project environment (3) you have to develop and implement up front a tracking and control system. It must be in writing, contain the necessary information, and be visibly posted. While numerous computer software packages can help you do this, don't overlook the value of a good, old-fashioned, low-tech metal scheduling board (speaking of *magnetic media*) that allows you to visually display the assignments and their deadlines. You'll find that those metal boards have one advantage over software: their physical size calls attention to the content, and can serve as a subtle—or not so subtle—goad to performance.

Using visual management. This technique, by the way, has a formal name: visual management. Studies show that an organization or department gains 20 percent performance improvement through the act of regularly and formally displaying key productivity indicators in a visual manner. Visual management is relatively low key, unambiguous, and easy, as well

---

Using Teamwork with Individual Work

Set up a *buddy system* in which each person has a designated *buddy* for advice, coaching, or just as a sounding board. Rotate relationships regularly.

Arrange for people with less-developed skill sets to understudy people with greater mastery. Follow up to make sure that learning and support take place.

Set up group meetings to discuss individual assignments with the goal of offering advice, pointers, and tactics to improve everyone's productivity.

Use *brainstorming in a circle* to bring the group knowledge to bear on individual project problems.

Provide regular and consistent feedback to all team members, making sure not to neglect the self-contained peak performers in favor of the problem people.

Make cross-training a key goal if the skills in your team are readily transferrable. In cross-training, people learn jobs other than theirs, benefiting the department and the individual simultaneously.

---

as relatively inexpensive to implement. Identify your key performance indicators (deadlines, milestones, quotas, financial goals, and so on) and post them, along with regular updates. You can use metal board systems (check any good office supply catalog to find numerous ready-made options), printouts from various computer programs, or even poster boards with magic markers. Look for ways to present information graphically, not numerically, and focus on displaying information in a way that communicates your goals (4).

Using teamwork in an individual structure. Although it seems somewhat redundant, look for collaborative and teamwork opportunities even in an individual work structure.

- Although individuals may do most work, some work and special projects may require teams.
- Individuals need some degree of cross-fertilization of ideas, advice, and inspiration to achieve maximum productivity.
- You need other people to know how to pick up work midstream in case of staff turnover or long-term absence.
- You need to provide regular internal ways for team members to acquire new skills and grow in work maturity.

You'll find some ideas for self-directed work teams (SDWT) are useful even in an individual work structure. Some specific tips are given in the sidebar, *Using Teamwork with Individual Work*.

Brainstorming in a circle. Each team member writes a current problem on the top of a piece of paper and puts it on a clipboard. In the brainstorming session, each participant passes her clipboard to the person on the left. That person writes five ideas or suggestions to help with the problem. Then clipboards are passed left again, and the person writes five additional ideas, and so forth until the clipboards have made it back to the original person. With five people, each participant will come away with twenty suggestions (four other people times five ideas/person) for solving her problem.

Thirteen Characteristics of Effective Work Teams

1. Trust
2. Empowerment
3. Authentic Participation
4. Ability to Manage Conflict
5. Basic Communications Skills
6. Use of Delegation to Help Others Learn
7. Willingness to Embrace Innovation, Creativity, and Risk Taking
8. Leadership
9. Decision-Making Skills
10. Integration of Personalities
11. Need for Constructive Change
12. Goals and Objectives
13. Training

Source: Temme 1996, 9–15

Specialist Group Structure

A specialist group structure is appropriate when the job is work (as opposed to project) oriented and teamwork is necessary. In a pure specialist group, each person possesses a different skill set with little or no overlap in skills, and often also brings a different perspective to the work. An example might be a customer-support team consisting of engineers, programmers, and sales/marketing specialists working together to service a customer site or installation. A group of specialists may have overlapping skills (a programming or engineering team, for example) as well, and still use this structure.

This is a classic team structure, and quite a bit of literature exists on both developing and managing with this structure. You may also be working in an organization that has made a commitment and focus toward developing a *team culture*, and you may therefore receive some pressure to go with this approach.

Key Traits of Effective Work Teams

Teaming authority Jim Temme identified key traits of effective work teams, which are featured in the sidebar.

From the long list in the sidebar, you can quickly notice one thing: achieving good team performance is neither automatic nor free. One reason that teams and teaming don't always enjoy a positive, noncynical reaction from prospective team members is that the process can be difficult, is often time consuming, and is not automatically guaranteed success.

The Development Life Cycle of a Team (Tuckman Model)

Forming
Storming
Norming
Performing
Adjourning

Source: Kormanski and Mozenter 1987

Stages of Team Development

Even successful teams go through a development process, and the stages are fairly predictable (see the sidebar).

Forming. It's unrealistic to expect teams to go from zero to sixty instantaneously. How you get the team structure started is important. In the forming stage, the first step is to set goals for the team. These goals involve several different elements:

- Determining the organization and departmental mission, vision, and values and how this team will contribute to meeting them.
- Setting a specific mission and purpose for the team—including roles for the team and its members—that are compatible with the mission.
- Setting rules and policies for the actions of the team and its members in areas such as conflict resolution, meetings performance, giving and receiving work assignments, supporting other team members, and so on.

The goal of the first stage is awareness of the team concept. The outcome of the stage should be commitment to moving ahead. The relationship outcome should be acceptance of team members.

Storming. It's often the case that different team members see the goals and reasons for the team's existence differently, which produces conflict. Even when the team members start pretty much on the same wavelength, there's often disagreement on the details of who does what and how it is done, which produces conflict. Conflict, dissension, possible senses of futility, individuals who haven't bought-into the concept—this is the storming phase.

The trick in managing conflict is first to see it as essentially positive and necessary. And it is—if you look at it right. Whenever two or more people disagree, they are in conflict. While the conflict can result in anger and negativity, the worst thing to do in most cases is suppress the conflict only to have it come out in inappropriate work behaviors. Instead, making conflict a constructive activity means helping people learn ways to express contrary opinions and negotiate consensus solutions in ways that support the work, not damage it. The method of principled negotiation developed at the Harvard Negotiation Project involves learning skills to decide issues on their merits rather than through haggling. Look for mutual gains when possible, brainstorm to identify creative solutions, and apply strategies of consensus building so that people walk away feeling, at a minimum, that their essential needs have been met (Fisher and Ury 1981, xii).

In managing the storming process, focus on training and development activities. Be less concerned about immediate productivity benefits; the team members need to learn *how* to work together before they *can* work together.

The theme of this stage is conflict. The task outcome should be clarification of goals and direction. The relationship outcome should be a sense of belonging.

Norming. In the norming stage, the team members begin to work as a team, establishing internal rules, standards, and a culture. The team begins to set plans and procedures for accomplishing the work, and starts the process of doing the work. As a manager, you should be slowly removing yourself from the primary decision-making and supervisory role. In earlier stages it's sometimes necessary to provide strong and specific leadership to get things moving, but if you continue to provide that, the team never gets to try its fledgling wings.

The theme of this stage is cooperation. The task outcome is involvement in the work. The relationship outcome should be mutual support.

Performing. If you've made it through the norming stage properly, the group has turned from a collection of individuals into a true team: it has reached the performing stage. The team members are taking responsibility for decision-making, problem solving, conflict management, and goal achievement. The manager moves into a comparatively hands-off role as counselor and adviser. In fact, the team often gives the manager instructions or tasks, such as gaining permission, obtaining resources, negotiating with other department heads, and so on.

The theme of this phase is productivity. The task outcome is achievement. The relationship outcome is pride.

Adjourning. Different teams have different life cycles, and it's important to remember, given the emphasis on teams you find in many organizations, that teams aren't important for their own sake, but for the sake of the work. If the teams have been established for the sake of ongoing work, the teams may be permanent in nature. If the team has been set up for a specific project, a quality improvement mission, or a specific customer, when the reason for the team is gone, the team should put itself out of business, and the members should move on to other work or other teams.

Don't just put a team out of its misery; instead, the team should formally wrap up its mission, provide final documentation, identify lessons learned and problems solved, and perhaps even provide its own commendations and recognition to members and others in the organization that helped it succeed. This is called the adjourning stage, and not all teams go here.

The theme of this stage is separation. The task outcome is recognition for performance. The relationship outcome is satisfaction for a job well done.

Leading organizational development expert Marvin R. Weisbord identified three success criteria of a successful team (1990, 301):

1. The team resolves important dilemmas, often ones on which little progress was made before.
2. People emerge more confident of their abilities to influence the future.
3. Members learn the extent to which output is linked to their own candor, responsibility for themselves, and willingness to cooperate with others.

Barriers to Team Culture

Achieving a working team structure means identifying and overcoming the internal barriers that resist this kind of change. The key obstacles in most organizations are:

- Unrealistic employee expectations
- Lack of access to information and data
- Lack of access to and training in tools and equipment
- Inappropriate incentive systems for goals
- Lack of knowledge and understanding about organizational mission, vision, and values
- Deficiencies in skills and abilities related to work and team processes
- Leadership failures on the part of the organization and management.

By effectively addressing leadership issues, you can start the process of overcoming these obstacles. The four elements of your leadership approach must be: planning, communications, resources, and training.

Planning means defining in advance your goals and objectives regarding teams and teaming. Why do you want them? What will they do for you? What issues and problems do you expect?

Communications not only involves two-way sharing about goals, objectives, and problems, but also the fundamentals of working together. Poor communications behavior has probably doomed more teams than anything else. Communications issues involve ways to have better meetings, resolve conflict, build consensus, and convey facts and information in the directions up, down, and laterally.

Resources are critical. If people don't have access to the tools, equipment, money, and other resources necessary to do the job, then the job won't get done, and the morale of those tasked with the job will suffer. Perhaps you're in the common situation of being asked to do more and more with less and less, and you don't have the resources yourself. Welcome to one of the core challenges of leadership: your ability to persuade and negotiate sufficient resources by working with your own management. That's the core skill of office politics, a necessary part of your new job description.

Training needs to be continual and regular. The goal of training is to change skills, attitudes, and knowledge. Skill building often involves on-the-job training; it is always aimed at practical, specific, measurable results and is often customized to the exact methods of the organization. While technical training is usually skill training, other types of skills also provide productivity gains. Better communication, conflict resolution, negotiation, and other *people* skills all result in improved productivity because people must relate and get along to get the job done. Technical skills can be viewed as the engine. People skills can be viewed as the oil that makes the engine run smoothly.

Team member *attitudes* dramatically affect performance. If team members have a negative attitude about the organization, the work, or management's commitment to quality and change, simply providing skills training will have little impact. Training is an element of empowerment. People who don't regularly expand their scope of understanding cannot perform in an outstanding manner, and therefore can't be empowered.

It's often not enough to train skills unless the theory, context, and background are offered as well. Improving quality is not just about getting team members to accomplish the work better; it's also about getting the team members to understand how what they do affects the total quality of the product or service for which they are responsible, and what outstanding quality means to overall competitiveness and success for the organization.

GREAT Teams

A powerful tool for looking at team structure and team effectiveness involves the acronym GREAT (Dobson and Dobson 1997, 13–16):

Goals
Roles
Expectations
Abilities
Time

Goals. Teams need clear goals and direction in order to have any chance for success. It's never sufficient to stick five people in a room and announce, "Be a team." A key element in setting goals that work is to involve the team in the goal-setting process. Try having a candid dialogue about some of the frustrations and problems, focusing on possible solutions. (Beware of the cynical team member who wants to argue that there are no solutions and any attempt to change is doomed to fail.)

Roles. Another problem in making teams work is the practical and legitimate question, "What exactly are we supposed to do anyway?" Roles need to be clear and specific. What will the team do? What will it do that people weren't already doing? What will each member of the team do? What will you do? How will you determine whether people are doing what they're supposed to do? How will you deal with overlaps among responsibilities?

Expectations. How will you know if the team is working? What exactly do you expect to happen? What do team members expect to happen? What do they expect of you? What do you expect of them? What level of performance will you judge to be satisfactory? What outside factors might affect the ability of the team to achieve its goals? Are there interim performance standards that the team should meet on the way to achieving peak performance levels?

Abilities. The abilities of the team to do the work are made up of several elements: individual technical skills, interpersonal and communications skills, skills in team process, and knowledge and understanding of organizational and customer dynamics that affect the work. At what level are these abilities now? At what level do they need to be in order to achieve the goals? Are problems or ability gaps shared among team members, or are specific team members contributing more than their share? What steps can you, the team, and individuals take in the development of the necessary abilities?

Time. What timetable is appropriate to see the beginnings of improvement? How long before you would expect to see the team functioning at the desired performance level? What would be the early warning signs that change isn't happening as fast or as well as desired or planned? What backup steps can you take in order to make it happen?

It's important to remember that these questions aren't for you alone to answer—members of the team must answer them as well. If you plan to hold on to all the standards and major decisions, you aren't in the business of building a team that works.

Team building, according to Weisbord, succeeds under four conditions (1990, 299):

1. Interdependence. The team is working on problems in which each person has a stake. Teamwork is central to future success, not an expression of ideology or *ought to*.
2. Leadership. The manager wants to improve group performance enough to take risks.
3. Joint decision. All members agree to participate.
4. Equal influence. Each person has a chance to affect the agenda.

Why Some Projects Fail ... and Others Succeed

Five Reasons for Failure

1. Lack of Project Manager Authority
2. Lack of Team Participation
3. Bad Reporting
4. Lack of People Skills
5. Unrealistic Goals and Schedules

Three Reasons for Success

1. Committed Teamwork
2. SMART Goals with Real Consensus
3. Use of Project Management Tools as a Means, not an End

Project Team Workgroup Structure

Many of the same rules for team development apply to the project team structure. The core difference between a project team and a specialist group or work team is that projects end. Project teams, by their nature, are temporary and normally focused on a narrower, more specific goal than work teams. Because their deadlines are often definite and tight, they may have more trouble going through the stages of team development because there isn't enough time to allow the team to form naturally.

Involvement from the Beginning

One of the first rules for making a project team successful is to involve team members from the beginning—in fact, delegate to them significant elements of putting together the plan. If you're not skilled in the discipline of formal project management, now is the time to learn; you can't manage technical professionals for very long without also being an effective project manager.

Teach the Skills of Project Management

To learn anything well, teach it to someone else. You'll discover that the more skilled your team members become in project management, the easier your job will be and the more success you'll have in accomplishing project goals. Teach them everything you know about project management, then go out and learn some more so that you can teach it, too. Let members with some previous skill share their knowledge and inside tricks to improve everyone's skill, especially your own.

Every member of your team should learn how to put together a work breakdown structure, a Gantt chart, and a PERT chart. They should participate actively in estimating and planning their own work. Use visual management techniques by displaying plan documents prominently in the work area.

Organizational and Customer Dynamics

Projects are difficult to manage for two reasons: projects take place within organizations, and projects have customers. Both organizations and customers consist of people. People have different interests, goals, and styles. People don't as a rule check their humanity at the door when they punch in on the time clock. The project outcome they desire always has an emotional and personal content as well as a measurable and objective content. While the political aspects of projects may be a source of frustration (and occasional despair), you must develop strategies and tactics to deal with the real world of project management.

Exercise 16

Team Issues for Projects

1. List the resources (people, tools, systems) you need to accomplish the project goal. Specifically, how much official control do you have over each resource?

   _____
   _____
   _____
   _____

2. Do you select your own team members, are they selected for you, or is there a hybrid responsibility?

   _____
   _____
   _____
   _____

3. Does each key member of your project team report to you in a formal sense? If not, what level of authority do you possess (able to fire, reprimand, dismiss from team, and so on)? Do any members of your project team outrank you in the normal office hierarchy?

   _____
   _____
   _____
   _____

4. What is the skill level of each team member? How do the skills fit the project goals? What skill deficiencies exist? How will you deal with them?

   _____
   _____
   _____
   _____

5. How well do team members work together? Are there personality, mission, or value conflicts with which you will deal? Do people have acceptable communications and people skills?

_____

_____

_____

_____

_____

6. What level of project management skills do your team members (and you, for that matter) possess? How will you upgrade those skills, and in what areas is that important?

_____

_____

_____

_____

Debrief of Exercise 16

Start thinking about the team issues on your project. Take the time to write fully your answers to each question, using extra paper. It's important to write this; you'll see it more clearly and be able to use it more effectively if it's in black and white.

Where you have identified gaps between necessary and desired skills, start thinking about ways that you can fix them, either by training, coaching, or changing team composition. Where your own skills are deficient, what steps can you take to improve them yourself? Who can help?

Don't feel you need to solve your problems by yourself. Call in your boss and others in the organization, and ask for help.

Selecting Team Members for Projects

While the reality of project management is often that your team is a given, it's clearly ideal to select team members strategically. Even if you have limited power to select your team members, work through these issues. You may need to acquire certain skills outside the core team. You may also identify some likely management issues affecting team performance. You may not be able to solve all your problems in advance, but advance warning is helpful.

The two factors in selecting team members are skills and personality.

First, skills—the initial draft of the project team should help you determine the skills that you require. Make a master skill list. As you choose team members, check off their skills against your skill list. In the ideal team, you should have at least two people (one a backup) with each critical skill so that in the event you lose a key member during the project life span, you'll have options. Cross-training is useful; so is preassigning backups so that each team member keeps his backup abreast of critical details.

Second, personality—once you have ascertained that the prospective team member has the fundamental skill levels required to do the work, favor personality over additional skill, because the ability to work with others toward a common goal is more important than marginally improved skills in most cases. Is the person articulate? Assertive, rather than aggressive or submissive? Can the person attend a meeting and neither dominate it nor sit there like a bump on a log? Does the person have a strong work ethic? Does she understand and support the project goals?

Interview team members whether or not you control their hiring. Ask them about their backgrounds. (Even if you've worked with these people for years, you may be surprised at the skills they possess that have never been called upon in the current work environment. Does your boss know everything that you've ever done?) Ask them about their goals within the organization and within the project. (This is key to motivating them. To give people what they want, you must know what they want.)

Team Organization

This is influenced by the situation. Does your team need a formal structure with clearly defined authority and responsibility for each member, such as a construction project? Does it need an informal, ad hoc structure that adapts to changing circumstances, such as an R&D effort? Are the people in the same physical location, or are they spread geographically? Will they have a long-term working relationship, or are they together only for this brief project?

Self-Directed Work Team Group Structure

Maintenance and Innovation

What exactly should you be doing each day—management or leadership? While the definitions of management versus leadership vary, depending on who's writing about it, one quick guide is this (Imai 1986, 5–6):

Management = Maintenance
Leadership = Improvement

Management as a maintenance activity involves making sure that the work is done in a way that meets the standards: technology, quality, and procedures. Management develops the standards and policies, and assigns tasks and functions to individuals and teams, then makes sure that everyone follows the standards. If they can but don't, management provides discipline. If they can't, management provides training or changes the standard so that people can follow it.

Leadership involves improving the standards and developing people's abilities to follow those standards, both in terms of minor changes (continous improvement) and major changes (innovation, reengineering).

In the normal organization, the responsibility for maintenance and innovation functions changes as you move up the hierarchy. Workers are primarily responsible for the maintenance and execution of the standards, with only a small role in innovation; levels of management and supervision steadily change the ratio of maintenance functions to innovation functions, as shown in Figure 11.

Three different patterns showing this changing relationship are common in organizations.

In the traditional organization, innovation takes a back seat at all levels—even executive management is primarily involved in maintenance activities. Little or no innovation takes place. In a competitive and fast-changing environment, this is clearly a recipe for trouble.

A common phenomenon in the high-tech organization is the reverse: a major push at all levels for innovation, with little or no management attention given to maintenance. In the very short run, this can result in rapid growth and amazing innovation, but you already know

Roles of Management and Team Members

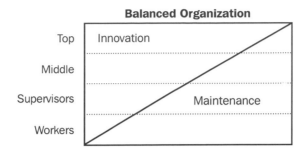

Balanced Organization

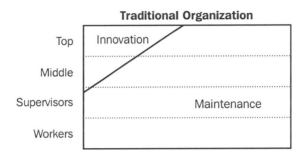

Traditional Organization

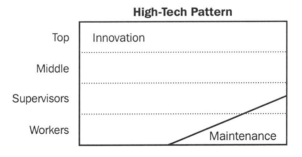

High-Tech Pattern

Figure 11   Innovation Model for Leadership

story after story of how yesterday's leading-edge company ended in today's bankruptcy court. Failure to attend to necessary maintenance activities can quickly become fatal.

The well-run company needs attention to both innovation and maintenance, both leadership and management. Properly, the levels of the organization make different types of contribution; the balanced organization shows good attention to both essential elements.

How can you best grow a fast-changing, high-tech organization? Obviously, you need to be able to turn more attention to leadership and innovation functions while making sure that maintenance is fully supported. The more that lower levels of the organization can take charge of maintenance functions and keep them going with good quality, the freer management is to exercise leadership.

That's the core reason why self-directed work teams (SDWT) are a popular goal in many organizations. The goal of an SDWT is for the team, gradually and over time, to take increasing responsibility for its own management (maintenance), and even for some self-leadership (innovation). Among the reasons why organizations resist developing an SDWT approach is the fear on the part of managers that if teams can manage themselves, the managers will be out of a job!

Middle management, as you already know, is an insecure position. However, leadership is secure, because when you are a successful innovator who gets results, you will always have a role to play.

The Self-Directed Work Team

Achieving an SDWT is easier said than done. Temme notes, "The key is this: power should be granted over time" (1996, 109). If a team, whether specialist team or project team, is to achieve self-management and self-direction, it must be empowered, which means real authority, access to tools and knowledge, clear goals, and the skill and training to use them in achieving organizational objectives.

The SDWT isn't fundamentally different from the team concepts that you've already covered in these pages; it's simply more, and it takes place over a longer period of time.

To turn your workgroup into a self-directed work team , start by implementing the basic team structure, following the stages of the Tuckman model, except for *adjourning*. Concentrate on the process of helping the team acquire and effectively use a growing level of decision-making power and authority on projects and tasks that grow in complexity and importance. Your goal is to hand off control and responsibility to the team as fast as it can handle it, until finally it is both able and willing to take over the maintenance/management functions of the department.

In the same period, you are altering your supervisory style through the four stages of the situational leadership model, until finally you have reached the fourth stage: low task, low relationship. The team is now on its own. You are a counselor and occasional coach, and spend your time in long-range planning, liaison, and innovation.

The SDWT format is a long-term goal. Even if you never achieve the textbook ideal, the more self-maintenance that your team can take over, the more time and opportunity for you to move ahead with the issues and innovation that concern you most.

Tiger Teams and *Skunk Works*—A Special Structure

In a study of fifty research laboratories, it was determined that smaller organizations often produced more innovative work per capita, some even achieving greater total output than their larger counterparts (Humphrey 1997, 184). Noticing this, even larger organizations have put together *skunk works* or *tiger teams*—small groups of eight to ten people, often in a physically separate location, responsible for getting the job done with little or no interference from company headquarters.

Tom Peters observed, "The places where we heard about skunk works tended to be those where more elaborate structures for supporting or encouraging champions did not exist" (Peters and Waterman Jr. 1982, 212). Innovative and excellent companies often set procedures and systems to support product champions, who serve as the advocates for getting great ideas through the system.

The development of the Macintosh computer was a more elaborate skunk-works project. Steve Jobs took a group of Apple engineers to a separate building, cut off from the main

Cupertino facility, and ran the Macintosh development program personally. Of course, once the Macintosh hit the market, the skunk-works team was folded back into headquarters.

While skunk works have much to recommend them, and their track record is undeniable, Richard Stein identifies three cautions (1993, 41):

- They disrupt and demoralize everyone else.
- They make progress and budget less plannable.
- They cost money.

Skunk works are most suitable where speed is critical, where the organization as a whole doesn't support innovation well, and where management doesn't plan and organize for innovation and achievement. The better solution is to work at developing the entrepreneurial spirit of innovation at all levels, and then, in a way, the entire organization acts like a tiger team.

Choices and Forced Choices

As a manager and leader, you have a varying degree of real power and authority in designing your own organizational structure for your team, department, or project, ranging from quite a lot to very little. Whether or not you call it a team, whether or not it is a team, you work with a group of people who have relationships and function organizationally as well as individually. It's much less important what you call it than what it does. The more successful you are at fostering self-development, empowerment, and excellence, the more naturally the group will form itself into a team and the more effective any structure will be.

Notes

1. Depending on the work maturity and organizational culture of your team, it may not be a good idea to refer to an IDP by its formal name; it smacks of *bizspeak*. You can easily use the concept without using the name, and make its implementation informal rather than official.
2. What you get on *Let's Make a Deal* if you pick the wrong door.
3. For more on this critical professional skill, see Dobson 1999b.
4. For good ideas on effective use of charts and graphs, see Freeman and Bacon 1990, 32–46 and 85–90.

Chapter 11
Power and People Issues

More Power!

One surprise that managers in general (and managers of technical professionals in specific) experience is the sudden realization that your staff has power—often substantial power. Staff members can make or break your career; they can promote you ... or get you fired. They do this through the unofficial organization, the level of their performance, their relationships with other managers, and their acquisition and use of the techniques and tools of personal power.

There are four main sources of personal power in organizations, as shown in the sidebar.

You'll notice that only one source of power is *official*—that is, rooted in your title and position within the organization. You automatically trump your team members only in the single area of role power; you gain additional power only through developing yourself in the other three areas. In those areas, your team members can easily acquire more power than you.

In order to manage your team effectively, you need to be aware of the real-world power dynamic so that you can manage it. This doesn't mean that you need to be afraid of your team members' acquisition of power; in fact, their power can be your asset if it's used in support of team goals. It does mean that you need to manage relationships with team members with more awareness of the relative power on both sides of the equation.

Developing your power isn't a negative act; it's a necessary act. Fortunately, most of the things that you need to do to develop your power position with your team and with the organization in general are legitimately supportive of organizational goals. Earning more respect, networking to build better relationships, and working on your communications skills, for example, are all appropriate ways to develop your on-the-job effectiveness.

The Four R's of Power

1. **Role Power**—the power inherent in job title, committee, or task force assignments; control of resources or paper flow; technical specialization; and so on.
2. **Relationship Power**—who you know, both inside and outside the organization; the type of relationship you have with them; your networking ability; your ability to *work and play well with others*.
3. **Respect Power**—Your reputation, knowledge, skill, and track record on major projects.
4. **Rhetoric Power**—Communications ability, personal persuasiveness, and negotiation skill.

Exercise 17

Developing Your Political Power (The Four R's)

The level of your power and authority is a function of your actual level and the level of your team members. To be in control of your organization, you must have power sufficient to accomplish your goals. In this exercise, you will analyze your team power and compare it to your own in the four key areas.

   Warning! Any time you write on a piece of paper about any potentially sensitive or informal matter concerning team members, do it at home, away from company space.

Role

   What types of role power do my team members possess (special decision-making roles; control of resources, information, or paper flow; memberships on task forces and committees; and so on)?

   _____
   _____
   _____
   _____

   What role power do I possess in my current position in the organization (title, official duties, signature authority, committee memberships)?

   _____
   _____
   _____
   _____

How could I expand my role power?

_____

_____

_____

_____

Respect

What types of respect power do my team members possess (major accomplishments, job knowledge, problem-solving skills, reputation for quality and achievement)?

_____

_____

_____

_____

_____

What level of respect power have I earned (major accomplishments, personal integrity, job knowledge, problem solving)?

_____

_____

_____

_____

How could I expand my respect power?

_____

_____

_____

_____

Relationships

What types of relationship power do my team members possess (mentors, networks, committees, professional groups, industry contacts, friends—or relatives—in high places)?

_____

_____

_____

_____

What relationships do I have inside and outside the organization that develop and expand my personal power and influence (mentors, networks, committees, professional groups, industry contacts)?

_____

_____

_____

_____

How could I expand my relationship power?

_____

_____

_____

_____

Rhetoric

What types of rhetoric power do my team members possess (persuasiveness, negotiation, listening, public speaking, group participation, writing)?

_____

_____

_____

_____

How good are my rhetoric skills (persuasiveness, negotiation, listening, public speaking, group participation, writing)?

_____

_____

_____

_____

How could I expand my rhetoric power?

_____

_____

_____

_____

Debrief of Exercise 17

The unofficial power dynamic in an organization is one of the essential realities about which you must be aware and stay aware. You can expand this exercise by analyzing the power level of your boss, others in senior management, your customer point of contact, and so on. By understanding their power, you're in a much better position to work with it in ways that are constructive and productive.

In-Demand Technical Professionals

One part of the reality of relative power has to do with what negotiation expert Roger Fisher calls BATNA: your *best alternative to a negotiated agreement*. This is the best you can do assuming no agreement is possible. The definition of power in a negotiation often becomes which side has the better BATNA—who has *walk-away* power (Fisher and Ury 1981, 101–11).

When you try to impose your will and direction on a reluctant technical professional, it's important to consider his BATNA. In other words, how easy is it for him to find a new position elsewhere? (This is a case of *respect* power, the extent to which someone's skills are valued by the marketplace.)

Obviously, people move from the current job for a variety of reasons, including but certainly not limited to disagreement about direction and goals. However, if you're afraid that your staff members will get up and walk out the door if you give them assignments they don't like, your power may be unacceptably compromised. It's important to know the real bargaining position and options of team members, and adjust your strategy accordingly.

Many technical positions are currently in high demand; for others, demand may be weak. Demand can also vary by region; if a person is willing to relocate, her options may be high; but if not, the options may be very much reduced. Even when demand for a technical skill is high, sometimes the skill must be packaged with other abilities, such as ability to work well with customers. As a result, the power of an individual team member to easily change jobs varies with circumstances; overall demand is not the only issue.

Managing turnover, then, is often an important element in the management of technical professionals, and for many organizations, it's a particularly challenging problem.

The rule of thumb about staff performance is that it takes a year to train a person to do a job well, and job burnout or the need to reengage happens in the third year. Mary Roznowski of Ohio State University, tracking 1,026 Generation Xers, found that four years was the approximate time in which someone was content in a job. She discovered that while happy workers are initially less likely to leave than disgruntled ones, after four years they are equally likely to leave (Young 1997, 3).

You can't eliminate turnover, and there are a limited number of strategies that you can use to manage or reduce turnover.

Honestly Assess the Workplace

The first strategy is to make an honest list of positive and negative characteristics of the workplace. The Pareto Principle applies to jobs as well: the best job in the world will be about 80 percent positive and 20 percent unpleasant. (It's when the ratios are reversed that you have a problem.) Consult your staff members when determining the positive and negative elements (though if you have a team of screaming negativists, you might want to approach this subtly, rather than holding a staff meeting), so that the list reflects how they see their environment, not just how you see it.

Based on your assessment, next take two steps: 1) look at ways to increase the positive and reduce the negative characteristics, and 2) compare the list of actual positives to a list of desired positives (e.g., What would your ideal job situation look like?), and look at ways to make change.

The attractiveness of the job situation has a significant impact on turnover—the point of leaving a job is to get a better situation, and the better the current situation, the harder it becomes to improve on it and the less the desire to try.

Focus on Positive Motivation
Review the ideas about creating a positive motivational environment for colleagues. In a national survey conducted by recruiters Robert Half International, "limited praise and recognition" was ranked as the primary reason why employees leave their jobs today—ahead of compensation, limited authority, and personality conflicts (Nelson 1996, 66).

People are not and never have been primarily motivated by money; top technical professionals are pretty high up in Maslow's Hierarchy of Needs, and appropriate motivators need to be chosen to have an impact.

Be Realistic about What Can't or Won't Change
Positive motivation and improving the workplace itself don't mean that you should Pangloss over the problems that exist. Twenty percent of even the best job is going to be dumpy and unpleasant, and you do your staff members a big favor by helping them learn and understand that the grass isn't greener on the other side of the hill. "Wherever you go, there you are," said Buckaroo Banzai (quoting the Buddha) in the eponymous movie. You'll find that employees with limited work experience compare their job situations not to other jobs, but to an ideal job vision that they will probably never experience.

Not sugarcoating and not lying will help people make realistic assessments of how they see the 80/20 split. People who can't live with the reality of your organization aren't going to make good long-term team members, regardless of their technical skills; it's often appropriate to agree to part on friendly terms. It's far worse to have the kind of employee who quits … but doesn't leave.

Show That You Fight for Improvement
You can't, won't, and shouldn't win every attempt for better conditions for your team, but you should show that you are a hardworking advocate with senior management, even at the expense of getting slapped down now and then. You don't have to fight for everything that the team wants; you know that it shouldn't get and doesn't need some of it. But you do have to show that you listen, care, and strive for improvement. Don't be surprised when your valiant efforts aren't greeted with the recognition and respect that they arguably deserve; failing to recognize this is all too often normal human behavior.

Help Management Add the Numbers
Turnover costs money in training, project overruns, and work not completed. Do some financial analysis of your work situation and the level of turnover you experience, and identify the cost of changes that would lower turnover (more money, better tools, more training options). If you can demonstrate in clear and logical terms how spending more money on your team, directly and indirectly, will profit the organization, you might just get at least some of the help and change you need.

Learn to Live With and Manage It
Turnover is going to be a fact of life no matter how many of these ideas you try. Track the life cycle of team members to see if your experience is similar to the previously cited four-year study. If you have a natural rate of turnover, you can adjust your structure to minimize its bad effects and even get the benefits. (Disgruntled and unhappy workers leave quicker than happy ones, and that's not necessarily a bad thing.) Here are three steps you can take:

Example

Positive and Negative Workplace Characteristics

Positive	Negative
Interesting Work	Unclear Direction
No Dress Code	Regarded as *Geeks* by Other Departments
Decent Pay	Don't Get Newest Equipment
Able to Use Skills Effectively	

- Promote cross-training and an understudy structure, which develops new people faster and keeps you from dealing with the *indispensable* employee.
- Develop a recruitment plan that brings new people in on a regular basis, trusting in staff turnover to keep your total team within staffing levels.
- Coordinate your goals and team member goals. If you want certain work done and the team member wants to acquire certain skills to make him more marketable, tie the two together.

Difficult Technical Professionals and Other People

"People are difficult," says difficult people expert Robert Bramson, "because it works for them" (1986). People choose behaviors and strategies that have worked for them in the past. While anyone can be difficult from time to time, certain people develop a full-fledged case of *OPD*: obnoxious personality disorder.

While certainly not all technical professionals are difficult people, the characteristics that make someone a successful technical professional can predispose her to difficult behavior that fits a predictable pattern. Difficult behavior is often simply normal behavior taken to extremes.

Real difficult behavior is behavior that continues after you have provided corrective feedback. If the behavior goes away, the problem is solved. Consultant Paul Friedman reports a study that identified the four major categories of resistance to corrective feedback (1991, 7–8):

- Apparent Compliance: Subordinate appears to accept negative feedback, promises to change, then reverts back to previous patterns.
- Discouraging Word: Subordinate refuses to accept the superior's feedback.
- Alibis: Subordinate transfers responsibility for problems elsewhere.
- Avoidance: Subordinate absents himself from the scene.
  Some common forms of difficult people you'll likely encounter are:
- Technical Wizard: "I know more than you do, and I'll prove it no matter what it takes!"
- Unyielding Perfectionist: "I could squeeze six more lines out of this 12,000-line program, making it even more elegant, and it will only take me another year!"
- Cynic Before Her Time: "Been there, done that, seen it all, and I know improvement is not possible, and I'm only twenty-three!"

Learning all the strategies for dealing with difficult people is a lifelong struggle, and one beyond the scope of this volume (1). Nevertheless, there are a few strategies you can employ immediately:

Analyze the problem in behavioral, not judgmental, language: Behavioral language describes objective and observable reality, preferably in quantifiable terms without negative connotations. Judgmental language is how you diagnose or view it. To get almost any sort of productive change, you must first be able to describe the behavior. There's no such thing as an *attitude problem*—attitudinal issues may cause a problem, but the problem itself is necessarily behavioral.

Separate relationship issues from performance issues: Fortunately, there's no rule requiring you to like someone in order to work with him. Nor do you need to approve of someone's bad behavior in order to recognize positive behavior from the same person. The more you can stay objective and treat the behavioral rather than the personal issues, the more powerful and effective you will be.

Disengage emotionally from behavior that sets you off: Count to ten, take a timeout, do some positive visualization. You won't be effective if you're so angry that you're out of control. Sometimes getting to you is the goal of the difficult behavior, and you don't want to give that victory.

Plan before you communicate: Organize your thinking on paper. Keep records of behavior that must be changed. "You complain all the time!" is an emotional statement less effective than a list of seventeen specific examples of complaining over the last two weeks. Sometimes the person isn't aware of the scope of her behavior—or thinks you aren't.

Orient yourself toward problem solving: Be clear in your own goals. You want and need to solve the problem in the best way you can. This allows you to structure the situation for negotiation, which may get more change than using your power (especially if you don't have that much).

Look closely at your own behavior and contribution: The situation is almost never completely one-sided; when you can understand and recognize your own contribution, even if it is in fact minor, the more you can control at least some of the behavior.

Be patient: People learn to be difficult over time because certain behaviors produce certain results. Some difficult behavior patterns are learned in childhood. Even if you do everything right, it normally will take significant time and repetitive attempts to get the change you need.

Be persistent: People who have acquired difficult behavior patterns have the power of habit going for them. You will have to be both persistent and consistent to maximize your chance of achieving results.

Managing People Who Know More than You (or at Least Different Things)

The reason this book began with self-assessment exercises is to remind all technical managers that they likely share at least some of the characteristics of their own team members—both positive ones and negative ones.

Eventually you will find yourself managing subordinates who really know more than you do, either in the primary technical area or in specialty areas of the work. There are two elements to meeting this challenge: 1) coping with your own reactions and resistance to the situation, and 2) dealing with the behavior and reactions of the more knowledgeable or able subordinate.

To deal with your own reactions, you need to take the following steps:

1. Realistically assess your knowledge, skills, and abilities and those of your staff on a regular basis.
2. Work at thinking positive thoughts about having subordinates with greater technical skills. They can take over work so that you don't have to worry about it.
3. Identify your own strengths and achievements. No one is all things simultaneously, but you have real strengths and abilities to get where you are. Celebrate those strengths.
4. Celebrate and publicly recognize the skills of your team members; it's good for you and may help reduce some of their crowing.
5. Develop and implement a lifelong learning program for yourself. Necessarily, your program should focus on the skills needed to help you meet your career goals, which means more emphasis on *soft* managerial skills; but it should also focus on keeping you technically up to date.

Second, learn to deal with the behaviors of your subordinates when they think they know more than you.

- Don't get into a fight about it; you both lose.
- Recognize their talents without being forced to do so.
- Develop learning goals for team members—there's never a point when it's time to rest on one's laurels.
- Recognize the individual talents of all team members, not just the official superstars.
- Focus on specific achievements rather than too general or nonspecific praise.

It's normal and expected that outstanding people will use this respect power source as a way to influence negotiations with you on work assignments, pay, and perks. By recognizing others' strengths and the developmental needs of top performers, you can spread this power around a little bit to help avoid being blackmailed and coerced by a top team member.

Managing *Generation X*

French economist Georges Anderla conducted an analysis in 1973 of the growth of information. Taking as his unit of measurement the known scientific facts of the year 1 A.D., he determined that the total knowledge of the world had doubled by 1500 A.D. (It had taken between 40,000 and 100,000 years, depending on the estimated age of homo sapiens, to reach the level in 1 A.D.) The next doubling took place in only 250 years. The rate of increase has followed a sequence (Wilson 1982, 29–32):

40,000–100,000 years	=	1
1500 years (1 A.D.–1500 A.D.)	=	2
250 years (1500–1750)	=	4
150 years (1750–1900)	=	8
50 years (1900–1950)	=	16
10 years (1950–1960)	=	32
7 years (1960–1967)	=	64
6 years (1967–1973)	=	128

Current studies suggest that the rate of doubling has moved past the every-three-years mark and is starting to hit an eighteen-month cycle. Does anybody really expect this trend to slow soon?

This unprecedented rate of change has profound consequences. Futurist Alvin Toffler says, "We have in our time released a totally new social force—a stream of change so accelerated that it influences our sense of time, revolutionizes the tempo of daily life, and affects the very way we 'feel' the world around us" (1970, 17).

Among the reasons age has been historically venerated is that the experience that accompanied age was of great value. However, in technological fields, the experience of age is frequently obsolete and irrelevant when it comes to the technical work itself. (Management and other human disciplines profit enormously from this kind of experience, however.)

Our technical workforce becomes younger and younger, and even if you're not actually very old, you may suddenly find yourself stroking your imaginary gray beard while some young stripling demonstrates technical wizardry on equipment that didn't exist in your youth. And there may only be five years of age difference between you.

Add to that the concept of generational cohorts, and you have a special management challenge: working with Generation Xers—especially if you aren't one of them.

Is Generation X really something different, or is this sort of categorization another form of inappropriate stereotyping? Historians William Strauss and Neil Howe observe that generations have in common that they experience major events at the same approximate age. For example, World War II was experienced by the very young as a period of tight protection, by rising adults as a period of adventure and national service, by the midlifers as a responsibility for leadership, and by elders as an opportunity for vision. Everyone of a certain age group obviously doesn't turn out the same way, but has at least had the same experience base (Strauss and Howe 1991, 34).

The Generation X cohort is of the type that Strauss and Howe call a "reactive" generation, growing up in a period of social unrest and disintegration, becoming as a result pragmatic, self-reliant, and untrusting of institutions of any sort (Strauss and Howe 1991, 317–34). Combine that with the new technical skill set that comes more naturally to those who grew up with it, as well as the reduced generational size (compared to the Boomers), and you have a significant—and specific—management challenge.

Some of the characteristics of Generation X workers, resulting from the economic and social climate in which they grew up, include (Filipczak 1994, 20–27):

- lack of loyalty and a skepticism about the value of corporate loyalty
- belief that all jobs are temporary and inevitably lead nowhere
- shorter attention span, translating into need for frequent change in job assignment and skill building
- sense that work and life should be kept clearly separate, resulting in greater tendency to compartmentalize lives
- resentment of being *managed*, but strong need for feedback
- greater *technoliteracy*, lack of fear or awe about technological change.

Accepting the fact of difference can make it easier for you to supervise and manage this group. What works? Interestingly, in spite of criticism of Generation X workers as lacking work ethic and loyalty, most of the same motivational techniques work with them as with other groups. The difference seems to be that Generation X workers are more resentful of poor management practice and more likely to rebel or leave than the older generations in the workplace. They see more choice available and find less value in loyalty and longevity, and therefore are willing to put up with less.

One Generation X member put it this way:

> Manage me by teaching me things. Manage me by showing me how to do my job. Manage me by getting me better tools. Don't manage me by sitting on me and giving me demerits because I'm five minutes late. Don't manage me by saying I can't be trusted to give the customer a 35-cent credit. Don't manage me by telling me that you know better than I do and, if there's information that's critical to my job, you will be the judge of when it's appropriate to tell me (Filipczak 1994, 26).

Parental divorce has struck this generation harder than any other American generation. In 1980, only 56 percent of all dependent children lived with two parents who were both on their first marriage (Strauss and Howe 1991, 324–25). As a result, in addition to the new management roles of leader, counselor, and coach, some management experts suggest that you need to take on some of the roles of a parent (Filipczak 1994, 25). Of course, this too is not unique to Generation X; most experienced managers realize that some parenting is typically part of the real job requirement of supervision.

The operative question is what kind of parenting and how much parenting is appropriate. Notice that approval and positive reinforcement is a traditional parenting technique that is also a standard recommendation for managers. Providing clear direction and boundaries is a traditional parenting technique that is also a standard recommendation for managers. A seminar participant once observed at the end of a day of supervisory training, "I learned a lot of ideas that will work for my six-year old … and I learned a lot in a parenting class I took that helped me manage my staff!"

Perhaps the most salient change is that organizations today have by necessity taken on some of the roles that once were supplied by communities. From health insurance to day care to employee assistance programs, both public- and private-sector organizations provide personal services to employees. The boundary has blurred. One surprise reported by many supervisors is the extent to which team members bring personal problems and life issues to them for advice, support, and listening. Some of this support is now part of your role, but considering that most supervisors are not trained counselors, tread carefully. One technique to help avoid trouble is making sure that you avoid the *supervisor-must-know-best* trap: "I can't advise you on this" is a perfectly legitimate answer, especially if you are able to provide a referral for help.

The good news is that Generation X employees naturally welcome real empowerment and autonomy, the opportunity to develop skills and long-term marketability, and the challenge of meaningful work. They adjust readily to change and eagerly embrace technological innovation. Notice that the same characteristics that drive a Boomer-generation manager to despair may well be the characteristics that are valuable for long-term organizational effectiveness in today's fast-moving age.

How Managers Create Problem Employees— and How You Can Avoid It

Whether your workforce is primarily Generation X or any other generation, certain behaviors provide positive motivation to get the job done, and others provide negative motivation. A 1994 survey identified ways in which managers damage employee morale (see Figure 12).

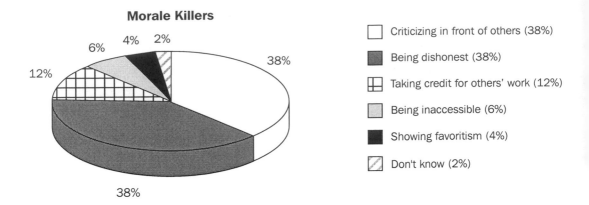

Morale Killers

- Criticizing in front of others (38%)
- Being dishonest (38%)
- Taking credit for others' work (12%)
- Being inaccessible (6%)
- Showing favoritism (4%)
- Don't know (2%)

Source: Fielder 1996, 41–43

Figure 12   Morale Killers in the Workplace

Motivation expert Barbara Fielder also identified these other behaviors that lead to workplace de-motivation (1996, 43):

- Delegating without giving authority, or delegating to the wrong person
- Communicating poorly or failing to communicate at all
- Failing to train employees for job responsibilities
- Exhibiting wishy-washy behavior
- Failing to emphasize teamwork
- Giving the impression that you're concerned only about your own well-being
- Displaying poor personal work habits, such as disorganization and procrastination
- Tolerating poor performance
- Oversupervising
- Imposing impossible workloads
- Focusing only on negatives.

If you're having trouble with team members, always take the time to look at your own potential contributions to your problem. Team members always look at you with greater focus than your own managers do, because your behavior more directly impacts them. While no manager is ever perfect—and most commit some of the earlier-mentioned sins at least on occasion—showing a willingness to take feedback and make a commitment to self-growth is one of the most powerful tools available to you to improve the morale and motivation of your team.

Notes

1. For more information on this subject, see the books by Bramson (1986) and Friedman (1991). Also see books by Deborah Tannen (1990), Suzette Haden Elgin (1989), and Virginia Satir (1988).

Chapter 12
Managing the Unofficial Organization

Office Politics and Newtonian Physics

As a manager of technical professionals, you have enough on your plate with managing yourself and your department or team. However, you have one more responsibility—one that will take an increasing amount of your time and talent: managing your relationship with the organization around you, including your boss, senior management, other departments, and your customers. This domain is known as the unofficial organization, and the skill you need for managing it is known as office politics.

Office politics, deservedly, has a bad reputation. However, there's a cleaner, simpler way to view the tasks and behaviors that you need. One is the understanding of the Four R's of power, covered in the previous chapter. Notice that acquiring power in this way is ethical and appropriate, because those are some of the same areas in which you work to increase your value and achievement within the organization.

Your official power is normally limited. Particularly if you manage projects, you must develop the skills to influence people over whom you have no official authority whatsoever.

To understand power, use the engineering definition: power that overcomes resistance to accomplish work. You need gasoline to power your car. Gasoline is morally neutral. How you get it is subject to ethical considerations. The car will run when you put gasoline in it—again ethically neutral. How you drive the car and what you do with the car are subject to ethical considerations. So is it with office politics and the acquisition of power. You need to acquire and use power to get the job done; your option is to acquire and use that power in an ethical way. Whether the power is formal or informal in nature is not, generally, a consideration.

Office politics is a reality in any organization employing three or more human beings. Office politics is simply the name we use to describe the informal and sometimes emotionally driven process of working out goals among people with conflicting interests. Many of the suggestions and ideas you've learned can be classified as *political* in nature, yet they are principled, appropriate ways to get things done. They benefit you, but not at the cost of hurting, manipulating, or taking advantage of anyone else or harming the organization as a whole.

You want to be an effective politician without seeming political. Some people give the impression that they are more concerned with their own advancement and who's doing what to whom than they are with the work and how to get it done. The effective and ethical manager demonstrates the latter consideration in thought, word, and deed.

While it's critical to be plugged into the informal information channels to make sure that you do understand what's going on, the concern you must have and show is that you are there primarily to get a job done and to achieve results for the organization. When that shows in your actions, the relationship building and negotiating activities that are part of effective politics are then seen as ways to contribute to the work.

What if you adopted the strategy of simply doing an excellent job and avoiding all political behaviors? Wouldn't your reputation and performance achieve the same results? Management experts Jerry Brown and Denise Dudley say no:

> Most [managers] would prefer to think that good work speaks for itself. Unfortunately, that policy is naive. Anyone out in the work force for a while soon learns that many factors other than ability or effort influence who obtains desired rewards and who achieves career advancement. … Company politics are a fact of life (1989, 63).

Managing Other Departments and People Who Don't Work for You

Virtually all managers quickly discover that they cannot get their jobs done without the willing and voluntary cooperation of people in other departments—people over whom they have no control or authority whatsoever. Few areas of your responsibility have as much impact on your overall success as a manager than your abilities to deal with other departments and to work the bureaucracy like a pro.

Your department may itself be either line or staff in nature. Information technology and management information systems are normally staff departments, because they don't make what the organization sells; they support the departments that do. New product development groups are clearly line departments, because they make what is sold.

The traditional source of conflict is between line and staff departments. Line departments in many organizations regard themselves as superior, more important than the support activities. Technically oriented departments are notorious for this behavior. The staff departments naturally become resentful, feeling (with justification) that without them the line departments would be unable to function, and that therefore they are as critical to the organization as anybody else—and they are right.

Even in organizations that are not torn apart with internal warfare between support and line, there is commonly an amount of normal friction with other departments. Everyone is busy, everyone has responsibilities and demands, everyone's resources are carefully monitored (especially in today's competitive business environment), and inevitably some conflict results. This need not be fatal, but you need to be aware of the potential for conflict, and act correctly.

Here are some common causes of conflict and potential solutions.

Work Pressures

If the key issue is work pressure, talk to the head of the other department as far in advance of your needs as possible. Emphasize that your goal is to do as much as possible to make it easier on him, even if it means some extra work on your part. Suggest designating one person as liaison; perhaps he can do the same. Treat the liaison as a team member—invite her to strategy and planning sessions where her expertise may be of help (any part of the project that involves the other department). If you have a party to celebrate the success of the project, invite your liaison (and possibly the department head). After all, they're part of your team.

Exploited by Other Supervisors

Staff departments in most organizations quickly learn that the claim by a line department that "the contract is at stake" is not always true. After a while, they begin to look at you as "guilty until proven innocent." Although you may well have a legitimate emergency, the support department has been abused in the past. In this situation, you sometimes see a particular saying appear on the cubicles of clerks in the support department. It reads, "A failure to plan on your part does not constitute an emergency on my part."

The only cure for this is time. If your attempt to be supportive to the other department is rebuffed, it may be because of long distrust and rivalry. Keep with your strategy, but be patient. You have to earn trust, starting from the guilty-until-proven-innocent position.

Negative Attitudes about the Organization

If the support department area has lots of cartoons and office sayings posted on the wall (e.g., the laughing workers with the caption, "You want it when?"; "I must be a mushroom. ..."), read them. Chuckle appreciatively, but realize that these sayings are funny precisely because they represent real frustrations and real pain. A staff department can easily decide that its contributions and hard work are not valued by the rest of the organization. This naturally leads to a negative attitude about the organization itself.

Line departments can also give up under too much pressure, too many projects, insufficient resources, or poor leadership. In some organizations where staff departments have a lot of power, line departments can feel unable to do quality work, and this frustration and sense of helplessness leads to negative attitudes.

You may not be able to change attitudes about the organization, but you can change attitudes about you. Follow the basic strategy, emphasizing the validation of people as people. Others will often do favors for you as a person that they won't do for you in your role as department head.

The biggest advantage you have in this situation is that the other department usually has a responsibility to do certain things for you, especially if it's a support department. A staff department, after all, makes its living providing services to other departments. If your situation is with a line department, normally the line department has a responsibility to provide some services to you. The R&D department has to give specifications to the manufacturing department, or else the product will not be manufactured.

Ultimately, the way to get other departments to cooperate is to treat them like customers. The customer/supplier relationship is a win/win relationship. The customer wants a product or service and has money. The supplier wants money and has a product or service. Everyone's needs are met. The supplier has to deliver quality, which includes how the customer is treated. If we want to meet the customer's needs, we have to do two critical things.

Find out what those needs are. That means we have to ask the customer what he wants and needs, why the need exists (so we can figure the best way to meet it), and when and how the needs must be met. For example, let's say the accounting department prints checks every Wednesday, and it needs one day's notice to get a new check into the batch for printing. Emergency check requests on Thursday are extremely disruptive. If you don't know how its system works, then you may easily create a problem for it ... and for you. How do you learn this? Ask. Make an appointment with the department head. Explain that you think you've been causing unnecessary stress on occasion because you don't know as much about the department's system as you'd like. Explain that you want to know how to work with it in the best possible way. Listen and take notes. Demonstrate your understanding by using the information that you learn next time you make a request or send through an assignment. When you demonstrate your willingness to work with the system, you will see improvement in the department staff's willingness to work with you.

Recognize customers as people. Courses in customer service always emphasize attitude as well as action. Of course we want to help a customer get what she needs. But how we treat the customer and how we show a positive desire have a tremendous impact on how the customer feels at the end of the process. "You get more flies with honey than with vinegar," the saying goes.

This does not mean that the way to get support from other departments is schmoozing. The professional technique isn't just to say, "How 'bout them [name of team]?" Recognize workers as people through polite courtesy—say "please" and "thank you." Learn the names of the individuals in the department and use them. Send thank-you notes to people who go above and beyond the call of duty, and copy their supervisors and the human resources department.

When negotiating specific projects or actions with the other department, work on creating a mutually beneficial agreement—a win/win situation. "What can I do for you that will make it easier for you to meet my needs?" is the core question.

Be prepared to go to higher authority if necessary to get your critical needs met. You want to avoid this until you've tried other steps. For one thing, people won't forget it. For another, your manager may perceive you as weak if you call for help prematurely.

Those concerns should not stop you if you must have cooperation on a timely basis in order to get your job done. Remember, part of the department's role is to help meet your needs. You'll be more effective when you appeal to higher authority if you can demonstrate that you have taken every positive step to get your needs met legitimately, and that you and your department have actively tried to be cooperative and supportive to the other department.

Managing Unclear and Escalating Objectives

Unclear Objectives

It's tough enough to do the work when you know what the work is. It's much tougher when you're expected to be telepathic.

A certain kind of manager or customer says, "Bring me a rock."

"What kind of rock?", you ask.

"A rock. Bring me a rock."

So you go get a rock.

"That's not the rock I wanted," you hear. "Bring me a rock."

"What kind of rock?", you ask again.

"A rock. Bring me a rock."

And so the circle goes.

Richard Stein points out, "This isn't freedom to choose your own work, this is just your boss not knowing what to ask for" (1993, 43).

One of the necessary political skills in an organization is knowing how to do your own intelligence work, which is the closest most of us can get to actual telepathy. Do you have your own internal spy network yet? In other words, do you have people who can—and will—tell you what's going on, what's behind seemingly strange requests, what people are really looking for?

The most dangerous words that can come out of your mouth are, "Yes, I'll do it," if said before you know what "it" is. The effective manager must be an effective consultant skilled at the questioning and research process to help his customers know what they want in the first place.

Escalating Projects

Projects acquire extra objectives and goals the way ships acquire barnacles. *Mission creep* is a well-recognized danger in the military, and the equivalent is common in organizations. It's normally not enough to have gotten agreement on the objective at the beginning of the work; you must revisit it periodically to make sure that it hasn't changed.

Remember that projects and work have customers, and those customers can be internal and external. Projects also often have multiple customers, and those customers don't automatically want the same things. Some customers can be hidden—they have a real stake in the work, but that stake isn't made clear at the outset.

As part of preparing to do the work, you need to take time not only on the technical activities to be accomplished, but also in the full and complete determination of your constituency. Who are they, what do they want, and what relative power do they have over your work? (Don't forget personal as well as external motivations.)

Exercise 18

Who Are My Customers?

Answer the following questions for each project.

1. Who is the main or official customer for the work?

   _____
   _____
   _____

2. What are the official objectives of the project?

   _____
   _____
   _____

3. What is at stake for the customer if I succeed or fail?

   _____
   _____
   _____

4. Who inside the organization assigned the project to me or to my department?

_____

_____

_____

5. What is at stake for that person if I succeed or fail?

_____

_____

_____

6. What other departments or activities inside the organization will participate in this project?

_____

_____

_____

7. What is at stake for them if I succeed or fail?

_____

_____

_____

8. Was this project previously assigned to someone else?

_____

_____

_____

9. Why was it reassigned?

_____

_____

_____

10. How will the previous person(s) be affected if I succeed or fail?

_____

_____

_____

11. Are any senior managers affected by the success or failure of this project? If so, who and how?

_____

_____

_____

12. Is there a constituency invested in the failure of this project? If so, identify who makes up the constituency, how they see that they will benefit by failure, and what power they have to influence that failure.

_____

_____

_____

13. Are there foreseeable situations that will change my project objective?

_____

_____

_____

Debrief of Exercise 18

Being realistic about the human dimension of the project is the necessary first step to dealing with potential conflict issues. If the issues you need to write about are politically sensitive or messy, do this exercise off premises.

If you find that you have people in opposition to the project, or people who see their interests very differently, examine the realities of the power situation. Enlist allies in your boss, customers, and others who will benefit from your success.

Finally, take these steps to avoid some of the dangers of mission creep.

Put It in Writing

A good goal is a written goal. Make sure that people are informed in writing in advance of the goal and given an early opportunity to challenge that goal. Although it can be difficult to negotiate a workable compromise, it's much easier than coping with a late-project major change order that virtually guarantees disaster.

Although people can still change a written goal, it's harder than changing an unwritten goal. As the famous Hollywood mogul said, "An oral contract is worth the paper it's printed on."

Document the Consequences of Changes

You can't take for granted that others in management will have the same level of understanding as you of the consequences of a proposed project change. Document the consequences of a change clearly and objectively.

When a change is requested, print a current plan and budget. Next, integrate the change into the existing schedule, and print the revised plan and budget. Third, brainstorm positive and proactive ways of achieving the new goal the best possible way. Revise the schedule and budget to accommodate the change.

Now, go to management and/or the customer. Show them the three versions: 1) no change, 2) integrate the change and keep going in a straight line, and 3) your best ideas about how to integrate the change and still achieve the rest of the time/budget/performance goals. Ask if they have better suggestions.

Perhaps they do have better suggestions—be positive and agreeable when you adopt them. Perhaps clearly seeing the consequences will make them realize that this is not wise or possible. It's easier for people to save face and back down if you're being positive.

Another point to remember is that management has a tendency to believe, based on much real-world experience, that employees don't tend to be proactive about change but instead look for ways to prove that change is impossible. Don't play into that preconceived notion; always be as positive as you can about change.

Build Change into the Process

In many situations, change orders are inevitable because of the nature of the work. It may not be possible to identify all the real needs until the work has progressed to a certain point. In this case, you need to build change into the process.

Set milestones in your project schedule for *customer review and expectation development* and tasks for *integration of requirements changes* and *redevelopment to accommodate changes*. Build this into your initial schedule and budget. If it's inevitable, it's inevitable. Plan for it.

Section Four
MANAGING TECHNICAL PROJECTS

This book so far has combined a discussion of projects—activities that are both temporary and unique—with regular (ongoing) work, because that's the normal situation in which the technical leader finds himself. But projects occupy a greater and greater role in organizations in general and in technical organizations in particular.

There are numerous reasons why this is true. The first is that today's organization must keep pace with rapid change merely to survive, and, like Alice's Red Queen, must run twice as fast to actually get somewhere (Carroll 1960, 210). Change involves projects, and projects require management.

Second is that project management itself has turned into the latest management fad (q.v.), and fundamental skill in project management and an organizational orientation toward project management are typically found in cutting-edge companies. While some work is unambiguously work and other activities are unambiguously projects, there's a fuzzy area in between that tends to be defined in project terms in a project management environment.

Third is that the tools of project management are far more accessible today than was true in years past (which is, not coincidentally, one of the reasons why project management—not a new discipline—is a new fad). When all planning tools had to be laboriously done by hand, it tended to take a fairly serious project for people to implement a formal project management methodology. With software tools automating what once took substantial time and expertise, a formal project management methodology makes sense on smaller and simpler projects than was once the case.

For all these reasons, you'll tend to find yourself managing projects in your overall leadership role, whether as a full-time occupation or, at the minimum, as a serious part-time job.

We'll assume that you already possess a decent background in formal project management methodology. If not, you need to be aggressive in seeking out those skills. There are a variety of books, training opportunities, professional organizations, and the like to help you in this process (1).

While all projects have challenges, uncertainties, and risks, technical (especially software) projects have certain specific issues that are often overlooked operationally, and which can have a significant impact on your effectiveness and ultimate success.

Notes

1. My own books, *The Juggler's Guide to Managing Multiple Projects* (Project Management Institute 1999b) and *Practical Project Management* (SkillPath 1996) are both examples of available resources, as are the extensive resources provided through the Project Management Institute itself (www.pmi.org).

Chapter 13
Technical Project Management Issues

Technical Projects and the Industrial Revolution

The breakthroughs in work process and methodology that formed the foundation of the industrial revolution included such concepts as standardization and mass production, and it's hard from our post-industrial perspective to appreciate how truly revolutionary these concepts once were.

These developments paralleled other ideas in science and literature. The cosmos was imagined to be a machine, working with a machine's regularity and process. The age of reason dominated literature, religion (God imagined as a watchmaker), and even poetry of the eighteenth century. Bureaucracy and the assembly line (see our earlier discussion of scientific management) extended the metaphor of the machine throughout society.

This kind of metaphor has power, and we end sometimes overinterpreting the metaphor, understanding it in a more literal fashion than is altogether appropriate. (Similarly, today we tend to overuse cybernetic metaphors, the concept of networks, of virtual this and that, stretching the metaphor into a reality that it cannot quite support.) As the noted semantician, Alfred Korzybski, famously observed, "A map is not the territory" (1958, 750). Metaphors are often extremely useful, but only as long as one does not take them to excessive lengths.

The problem with the industrial revolution mechanical metaphor when applied to technology projects, especially those in the area of software, is that there are important structural differences in the nature of the work. Those differences set up a clash of expectations and a difficulty in management that forms the basis of a substantial amount of conflict in organizations.

As you'll see, although the work on the cutting edge of technology involves some of the most advanced technical thinking of any work done today, the actual work process is pre-industrial, even medieval, in execution.

Characteristics of High-Technology Projects

There are three key characteristics of high-technology work that take it outside the traditional industrial revolution paradigm. These are:
1. Handcrafting.
2. Artisanship.
3. Nonreplicability.

Handcrafting

Software and advanced technology projects by their very nature fall outside the mass production paradigm. While there are some specific areas of software development that are fairly automated and standardized, most areas are not. The alternative to mass production is handcrafting—the individual design, development, and construction of ostensibly similar products.

In the absence of standardization, a table is not simply a table. While certain elements—a flat surface, some means of support—might be common to most tables, each craftsperson tends to approach the table from a different perspective. Dimensions, shape, decoration, color, methods of support—even aesthetics and functionality—may all vary.

Similarly, the software developer or development team approaches the project from a handcraft perspective. The goal may (or more frequently may not) be altogether clear, but regardless of its clarity, a wide range of methods and processes are normally available to achieve the goal, or some reasonable approximation of it. Moreover, the final product is expected to operate in a largely uncontrolled environment where conflicts are inevitable.

If you think of a software project in industrial terms, this implies some degree of predictability of process. "We will code an average of 200 lines per day, which will give us a 10,000 line program in fifty working days, with a variation not to exceed 2 percent." Of course, any such claim would be uncertain at best.

In an industrial process, you also think about predictability of method. Each team member is expected to approach her portion of the project in an identical method, so that the final machined products will fit together smoothly and on schedule. That's not necessarily a valid expectation in software or high technology. In fact, the integration of different modules is often a project in itself.

Finally, you think about predictability of results. The specifications for a construction project are often detailed down to the size of bolts used to fasten together certain components, so that regardless of the worker assigned to the task, you expect the same results. It's more reasonable to expect in a software project that if three workers should tackle the same section of the project, then there would be three distinctively different outcomes.

It's clear from our experience that none of these criteria apply, or, at the least, do not apply fully in the sphere of high technology. Not only does our problem as a project manager grow in complexity, but also our customers (both internal and external) often expect industrial revolution-style performance because the paradigm is so deeply ingrained in modern business thinking.

Solutions. Here are two strategies that flow from this analysis.

1. *Agreement on reality.* When one or more stakeholders on the project has a different view of the nature of the work process, it's vital that all parties come to an understanding of the realities of the project and technical environment. This means that you must be an effective advocate and persuader to help people who may be technically less versed or technologically more optimistic than you to come to an appreciation of the challenges ahead.

2. *Agreement on objectives.* A common problem in managing any project—but worse in technology projects—is a lack of agreement or consensus on what the goal is. Each project stakeholder (a person with some stake in the project's process or outcome) tends to have an individual view of the optimum outcome. Not all stakeholders are equal—some people have greater stakes than others; some have more power than others.

Triple Constraints. One conflict that often arises in the management of such projects is a fundamental disagreement about priority that flows from a lack of understanding of one of the most crucial yet overlooked elements of project management: the triple constraints (1).

It's not enough to simply accomplish the project. Rather, the project must be accomplished within certain imposed constraints, the most important of which are time, cost, and performance. The time constraint is the deadline, assumptions about timeliness, or sources of time pressure. The cost constraint is not only budgeted dollars, but also availability of resources. A person-hour is a cost issue, not a time issue. The performance constraint is the minimum performance criteria that the project must satisfy to be considered fundamentally acceptable.

It's typically a characteristic of these projects that the team members tend to set the performance constraint at the top of a hierarchy of priority, sacrificing cost and time in a drive to meet it. While in certain circumstances, that's exactly the right way to go about it, in other circumstances, those are the wrong priorities.

Let's imagine that you are developing the software to run the Winter Olympic Games. If you produce excellent software two months after the conclusion of the Olympics, it's essentially an irrelevant accomplishment. In this circumstance, the time constraint would be the project driver, the constraint that must be met or else the project has failed. Some combination of performance and cost may have to be sacrificed in other to meet the time driver of the project.

Sometimes—to the chagrin and annoyance of the technical team—cost is the driver. The budget may be limited, the number of bodies available to do the work finite, and other projects of higher priority have first call on available resources. It's inevitable that something has to give: some combination of time and performance.

Sacrificing performance on a project may result in a virtual mutiny by members of your project team, and that's a key challenge for the technical manager, especially when you secretly (or not so secretly) harbor a great deal of sympathy for their positions. But the project is what the project is, not what you would prefer that it be. Figuring the dynamics of the triple constraints on your project is critical to understanding what the objective or goal of the project really is.

Don't expect to determine the triple constraints and driver of your project by relying on the opinion of project team members, your own managers, or even the customers or stakeholders in many cases. First, they may disagree. Second, they may not know themselves. The priority of the triple constraints necessarily arises from the reason for the project—why are we doing this in the first place? When you understand the underlying reason, you're more likely to set the right priorities.

Artisanship

Artisanship is both pride and skill in one's craft, and it goes along with the handcraft nature of high-technology projects.

There are great positive benefits to an artisan attitude in your team members, but there are liabilities and limitations that go along with it. Your understanding of the characteristics of artisanship is one of the key elements that will govern your ability to manage projects effectively in a technology environment.

The positive elements of artisanship are many. First, artisanship tends to be associated with a reasonably strong work ethic. Second, artisans tend to have a strong focus on quality. Third, artisans are often motivated toward self-development and personal growth in the areas of their crafts.

On the other hand, artisans tend to resist supervision and requirements established by those who know less—even when the customer establishes the requirements. Artisans like to put their personal stamp on the work, to do things in the way they find best. Artisans seek personal control and independence in performing their work.

As you can see, there is a close correspondence between these characteristics and those we've associated with technical professionals as a whole. Our management challenge is to gain the benefits of the type while limiting the impact of the liabilities, or helping people to grow past them.

Solutions. In a significant way, the primary thrust of this book has been to identify methods to manage the artisanship impulse. Technical professionals aren't new; they are the proud inheritors of a long human tradition. What has changed is a growing emphasis on timeliness and a sense that resource limitations are human-set and therefore arbitrary.

In managing yourself and others, keep aware of the artisan impulse, keep focused on the work, but remember that the work is not an end in itself, but rather a means to an end. And, unfortunately, the technical team or its direct leadership does not always or necessarily determine the end.

Nonreplicability

Industrial and mass production processes emphasize replicability of results. If you do the same thing the same way, you will get the same output. Because in handcrafting a table is not simply a table but reflects an individualized approach, there is an inherent problem of nonreplicability in the management of technology projects. This is not to argue, of course, that nothing can be replicated, but rather to say that replicability cannot be taken for granted and is not always or necessarily the expected outcome.

Many of the traditional tools of project management assume predictability and replicability. If Task A must be complete in order to start Task B, then you create a simple task sequence, as illustrated.

If you can estimate the expected time for Tasks A and B, then the total time to complete Tasks A and B is obviously the sum of those times.

But in a development process, Task A may be a loop—we must perform the task again and again in an iterative cycle until we obtain a satisfactory result. We might be able to estimate how long it will take to perform Task A one single time, but it's an open question how many times the task must be performed before we can move ahead. How, then, can we come up with any sort of meaningful schedule?

Solution. In 1958–59, the United States Navy Special Projects Office worked on the Polaris weapon system with Booz, Allen, and Hamilton to develop PERT, the Program Evaluation and Review Technique. While PERT charting (or something passing for PERT charting) is a common feature of project management software tools, most smaller projects find that a full-blown PERT implementation falls under the category of driving carpet tacks with a sledgehammer.

However, PERT contains a very powerful technique, using probability theory, for estimating and developing a schedule under conditions of inherent uncertainty.

Let's look at the process.

Imagine that you're asked to predict how long it will take to do an original piece of software design where there are multiple possible approaches and no advance knowledge as to which approach is right for the problem—a not untypical situation for many R&D technical professionals.

It's possible that you will get lucky, and the first approach you select will turn out to be the right one—unlikely, yes; impossible, no. You can come up with a reasonable estimate for how long it would take, assuming first-time methodology success. Of course, you'd never use that estimate in putting together a schedule. We call the first estimate your optimistic value (T_o).

Similarly, you could assume that of, say, ten different approaches, the tenth one will be successful, and the other nine will be dead ends. Now, the reality is likely not going to be quite that bad, but it could be. Your worst case estimate will be your pessimistic value (T_p).

Most of the time, you'd assume that the right approach would not be the first or the last of the possible ones. (It will, of course, be the last one you actually try, on the grounds that whatever you've lost is always in the last place you look—because you will stop looking at that point.) You might figure that since you'll be putting the approaches in the order of likely payoff—to the best of your ability—that of ten possibilities, the fourth would be a good average value. That's the most likely value (T_m).

Is this process of any use? For a single task, no, it's not. But for a project with multiple tasks, it's relatively safe to assume that sometimes you'll get lucky, other times unlucky, and the majority of the time somewhere in between. You can express this as a formula solving for T_e, the estimate value for your schedule, thus:

$$T_e = (T_o + 4(T_m) + T_p)/6$$

Note that in the case of any individual task, the value T_e is not necessarily the expected or actual outcome. But by applying this formula to every task in the project, you begin to average the individual instances of good and bad luck, resulting in an estimate of greater validity.

The PERT time system has extended uses, especially when you determine the standard deviation for a task or task sequence in order to identify an overall level of confidence or likelihood of on-time completion (2).

Limitations and Cautions in Using Project Management Tools

There are three elements of being an outstanding project manager: technical knowledge, project management knowledge, and general management knowledge, as illustrated.

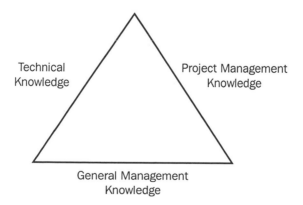

Technical knowledge is the knowledge of your profession, the understanding of the work itself. (Project managers have been known to be successful without possessing this in high degree, but it's clearly easier to do the work if you possess the knowledge.)

General management knowledge includes supervisory skills, ability to delegate, and knowledge of budgeting and organization and of your own administrative processes and procedures.

Project management knowledge involves an understanding of the various craft tools that have evolved to assist you in doing a better job of planning, organizing, and completing your project. Such charting techniques as Gantt, PERT, and critical path method; use of software tools such as Microsoft Project, Primavera, and FastTrack; and understanding of the triple constraints all fall into the category of project management knowledge.

Project management tools are valuable, but like all tools that help you be more technically proficient, there are traps for the unwary. Too many new project managers get a copy of a project management software program and find themselves spending their days inputting information and producing very attractive charts—but not managing the actual project.

Information Costs Time and Money

The first and most critical limitation of project management techniques is that managing with excellent time, performance, and planning data is quite advantageous—but it's expensive and time consuming. Project management scholar Harold Kerzner observes: "PERT, unfortunately, is not without its disadvantages. The complexity of PERT adds to its implementation problems ... [it is] expensive to maintain" (1998, 643).

This concern is not exclusive to PERT. In one case, a small advertising agency implemented a formal project management methodology to simultaneously control a large number of small projects—approximately 180 projects at any one time for a thirty-person company. Its challenge was to meet deadlines while controlling overtime costs.

The projects were highly specialized, with individual task packages as low as one hour. (This is highly unusual; most project management systems recommend task breakdowns no shorter than a day or even a week.) The company ended up with a two-person project control office.

A day-shift person supported the sales staff that sold multiple projects each day and needed to negotiate deadlines with customers. When a job was bid, the project control specialist would break it into tasks and insert them into the existing multiple-project schedule to see when it could be completed. This, incidentally, allowed the firm to offer discount pricing for customers willing to be more flexible on deadline performance.

A night-shift person took the actual sold jobs each day and entered them into the system, along with timecard data describing the task work performed during that day. The new schedule was checked, and from it individual assignment sheets were prepared and distributed to each person.

The costs of software and hardware were comparatively trivial. The real cost of this system was two full-time professionals totaling over $100,000 per year. Was it worth it? For this company, it was, because it resulted in more than a million dollars a year in overtime savings.

Project management systems have the potential to provide large savings and operational improvements, but the savings and improvements are not automatic; nor are they free. You need to have a fairly good idea how you plan to recover your sunk costs before committing to a high degree of information development.

Great information empowers better decisions, but information is not free and is not always guaranteed. Real-life managers, project and otherwise, are responsible for strategizing the right tradeoff level between the value of information and the cost of developing it.

Exercise 19

Nine Steps to Setting Project Objectives

It's almost always worth taking time and effort to thoroughly understand your project objective. Use these questions as a process to make sure that you understand fully what you're being tasked to do.

1. Identify the key project participants. (You may use your customer understanding from Exercise 18 in this process.)

   _____

   _____

   _____

2. Define the "rough draft" triple constraints of time, budget, and performance. Use the key project participants' language as much as possible; don't worry (for now) whether their request is reasonable or even possible. You need to know what you're being asked before you can evaluate it.

   _____

   _____

   _____

3. Analyze and develop any missing constraints. Your customer may not yet have thought about his budget, or exactly what the performance standards are, or what time issues affect the performance of the project.

   _____

   _____

   _____

4. Identify preliminary management issues. These include technical issues, reality checks, availability of resources, practicality of the desired or mandatory constraints, etc. The earlier in the process you begin to identify these, the more leverage you will have.

   _____

   _____

   _____

5. Examine the refined triple constraints to determine the likely priority among them. The priority ultimately comes from the reason—why are we doing this project at all?

   _____

   _____

   _____

6. Use your understanding of the project goal to refine the triple constraints and make a SMART (specific, measurable, agreed, realistic, time-specific) goal statement

   _____

   _____

   _____

7. Identify secondary and tertiary project goals—and who wants them. Remember that the larger the project, the more people who will want some of their goals and objectives reflected within it. Consider not only what these goals are (and what value they have), but also who wants them and what the consequences may be of accepting or rejecting these additional goals.

_____

_____

_____

8. Refine your project goals and test them with the affected parties. It's much easier to have a goal shot down than a project shot down.

_____

_____

_____

9. Revisit the triple constraints regularly throughout the project to keep yourself and your team focused. Keep your eye on the underlying reason or purpose of the project—if that should change, the project itself likely changes with it. Adapt early.

_____

_____

_____

Debrief of Exercise 19

One of the most common causes for project failure is a project whose objective was not properly defined to begin with. It's obvious that no amount of planning or insight will help you achieve a goal that is unknown, or perhaps doesn't exist in any meaningful form.

Most project managers spend too little time digging into the project at the outset. Too often, a substantial amount of the project has been completed before the project manager, customers, internal management, and team members figure what it is they are really supposed to be doing. By then, it's often too late, or it takes substantial time and resources to tear up and redo—or the project gets compromised to take advantage of what's been done and to avoid embarrassing waste.

You may not always get the most positive reaction when you try to get people to focus on these issues at the beginning, but you'll get far better results at the end.

Notes

1. For a thorough discussion of triple constraints and their application, see Dobson, Michael, 1996, 22–37.
2. For more: *ibid*, 104–16.

Chapter 14

Organizational and Customer Issues in Technology Project Management

The Alchemical Mysteries

Like medieval alchemists, technical professionals have been known to use smoke and mirrors or other obfuscatory techniques to cement their power and control and to promote the primacy of their areas of specialization. It's a human tendency, and one that can be too easily twisted to unprofessional and even destructive ends.

One theory about the origin of jargon is that when we make up a secret vocabulary about our career field, we get paid more. There's certainly a legitimate reason to create words necessary to define those concepts unique or special to a given technical field, but there's equally a tendency to go farther than strictly necessary to provide a sense of mystery and keep out the *great unwashed*.

This can result in a certain degree of macho posturing in technical project management. This posturing is not only on the part of technical experts and project managers, but also on the part of customers and other stakeholders, who, after all, have the human tendency to want to be *in the know* and use the *secret handshake*.

The desire to be part of the *technological cognoscenti* is the source of much project management misery, regardless of its source. Let's look at some sources and problems in order to develop solution strategies.

The Priesthood of Project Managers

A project manager is often appointed to that role because she possesses more specialized technical knowledge than the customer. A customer is not required to have knowledge; a customer simply must have a need.

Because we often know more than our customers about the work to be done, there is a tendency to believe we know more about the need—and while that is true in some instances, it's a dangerous supposition to make. The consequence often is that we deliver over-elaborate solutions to simple problems, or, worse, solutions to problems not in evidence because they're technically elegant.

Solution. Adopt a customer-centered attitude to your role as a project manager. Project managers are hired hands; we exist and are employed because we solve other people's problems and fulfill others' needs through the application of our technical and managerial skills. If your customer is not as technically sophisticated as you, it does not make your customer inferior, ignorant, or ill informed. A project is only successful if the customer believes that his need was met. If you think you've solved the problem, but the customer disagrees, you still pay—you may not get repeat business; your reputation is not enhanced.

This implies developing a personal relationship with the customer, something your organization does not always or necessarily support. Nevertheless, you must develop one in order to achieve first-rate project management results.

First, invite yourself into the leadership group to seek direct customer contact. Sometimes this works, even if it's not customary in your organization, on the general theory that initiative counts. If that doesn't work, try asking or negotiating for at least limited customer contact, explaining how it's beneficial to the organization. You might try discovering the rationale for limited direct technical contact with customers. There may be some good reasons—technical professionals sometimes try to dominate the dialogue inappropriately, or do not present themselves in accordance with organizational values. If specific reasons exist, you may be able to demonstrate that those reasons don't—or shouldn't—apply to you.

Next, try to recruit your own parallel intelligence network from among those who do have direct customer contact. Don't take any single source of information as gospel; people naturally filter information based on their own points of view.

Finally, if you aren't able to get good customer contact for this project, do your very best anyway, but keep a log of issues and problems that would have been resolved more quickly or better had you been able to work more directly with the customer. Use this information to build a case for long-term change.

"Tim (the Tool Man) Taylor"ism

"More power (grunt, grunt)" is the mantra not only of some project managers, but also of certain customers. The actual need may be modest, but the proposed or desired solution is at the cutting edge of technology.

There is a *toy value* that goes with many technological solutions. In many companies, see who has the most loaded laptop: someone who actually spends her day working with the computer, or a senior executive who seldom uses anything beyond the word processor, spreadsheet, or email functions (1)? If it's the latter, you've identified a situation in which technology is purchased at least in part because of its inherent toy value—and, as most technical professionals know, "he who dies with the most toys wins."

How often are projects launched in your organization not because of an actual need, but rather in a competitive desire to be first on the block with the latest and greatest toy? Or, if there is a real need underlying the project, how often are the technical means chosen because of their *coolness* rather than whether they are fit for the task at hand?

Obviously, this tendency, if unchecked, results in substantial waste, products or projects that don't achieve benefits, or ones that achieve benefits at unacceptable cost or complexity.

Solution. Arguments about the right level of technology for a project often revolve around the question of quality. A less complex or robust solution is accused of being *low quality*. Rightly, no one wants to be perceived as being *against quality*; so the question becomes: "What is quality?"

Fortunately, quality can be defined in a fairly rigorous and objective manner. It doesn't have to be the fairly fuzzy *more is more* concept that it turns out to be operationally in so many cases.

As we discussed earlier, there are two major schools of thinking about quality. The first (W. Edwards Deming, et al.) is customer-centered quality—quality involves meeting or exceeding customer expectations. The second (Philip Crosby) is that quality is conformance to requirements.

The limits in both concepts are fairly clear. In Crosby's definition, what if the requirements as defined are faulty? You can do exactly what you've been tasked to do, and yet have an unsatisfied customer. Your repeat business is limited, and your reputation suffers. Who determines the requirements, and why is their judgment any better than your own?

On the other hand, Deming's standard must necessarily be developed at a higher level of the organization. It's not always clear how quality at the detail level relates to customer needs, especially from the point of view of the person who must do the actual work. Customers may be vague or mutable in their own understanding of needs—they may not know what they want, but they can always tell when you haven't delivered.

Ideally, what we seek is a feedback loop leading to a fully validated definition of quality. First comes the understanding of the customer, and from that flow detailed requirements. The requirements, in turn, can be linked directly back to customer needs. At each level of the project, people know what they are to do, how much is enough, and under what circumstances more isn't necessarily better.

Orient yourself and your project team toward an operational definition of quality, and you'll find it easier to build consensus on using the right tools the right way to accomplish the right job.

Between Scylla and Charybdis—The Challenge of Multiple Projects

If it hasn't happened to you already, it's only a matter of time before you have not one but multiple projects. And it's shortly thereafter that you first discover that managing multiple projects isn't merely quantitatively different, but it is also qualitatively different (2).

Issues of quality raise their heads here as well. When you have a single project, you can—and normally should—focus on achieving the best quality. When you have two projects, you normally feel some competitive strain, but through dint of hard work and creativity, you can often get both jobs done without forced compromises.

But what if you have five? There comes an inevitable point where the willingness to work hard is not enough. Something has to give. You can't control multiple projects to the same level of detail and performance as with a single project.

Areas of conflict abound.

Conflict Areas in Multiple Project Management

Because there is inherent and unavoidable tension when you are in a multiple project environment, you should analyze your portfolio of projects for the most common conflicts, because advance understanding expands the available options.

Case Study 12

Baby Killing

"When we were rich, we acted rich," observed Günter, a newly promoted new products manager. "That meant projects selected not because of market potential, but because of the interest or enthusiasm of specific engineers. When we became poor, things had to change."

Günter inherited a product development schedule from a disgraced predecessor and was given his marching orders: everything had to be completed; no products could be cut from the schedule.

"The first thing I did, of course, was cut product," he laughed.

When you're faced with an absolute such as this, and the absolute seems to take away any options you might have for successful completion of your project, look for the reason underlying the absolute. In this case, there was an assumption on the part of management (and the company's creditors) that products equal revenue and profit, a reasonable enough assumption under most circumstances. However, in this case, some products that were not even potentially profitable were on the schedule; they were being pursued almost as hobby interests on the part of certain engineers.

"When I could show that completing these projects meant we'd lose money, I was then able to get them cut from the schedule. Of course, that was the easiest part of the problem," observed Günter.

The harder part of the problem was the entrenched attitudes of the engineers whose pet projects were being threatened. "It was essentially as if I was killing their babies," he said, "and they reacted accordingly."

You might assume that in this case you should expect and require your subordinates to fall in with the company strategy—and to some extent you should. On the other hand, having a privilege taken away is often worse than having never had it in the first place. This is a recipe for creating enemies, demoralized and unproductive staff members, and even a climate for sabotage.

"Although this was a necessary action, the feelings of the people losing their pet projects was going to have a direct impact on the department's other work, and I couldn't afford to jeopardize that," he said. "I felt I had to confront the situation directly and resolve it through negotiation."

Such a negotiation involves two separate issues: the emotions and the facts. While you should try to keep them separate, both are important, and both must be resolved in order to achieve your goals.

"I knew that one project in particular was very precious to one of my engineers, and I was letting him design something really cutting edge. Unfortunately, there wasn't any commercial potential. So I set up a private meeting with him and explained what I was going to have to do. He gave me the silent treatment; if looks could kill, I would have been fried. I let it go for a few minutes, and then tried some empathy. 'I can see you're very upset. If I were in your shoes, I'd feel that way, too. I'd be thinking about this

continued on next page

Case Study 12

Baby Killing (con't.)

newly promoted lowlife who comes in and immediately tears out everything that was worth working on, how outrageous and unfair it was. … ' I kept up in that vein for a few minutes, because I really did understand how he felt. Finally, he exploded: 'So you think you understand? Listen, you @#$%. … ' Normally, I don't think it's a good idea to encourage your staff to swear at you, but this was a special case. I needed to lance the boil, and that's what I did. I let him yell and let off steam for a while and didn't react—though it was difficult. After a while, he began to calm down.

"'So, we've got a problem,' I summarized. 'What should we do about it?'

"He glared at me, and after a pause, said, 'You owe me one, big time.'

"'Okay,' I replied. 'What do you want?'

"'I want my pick of projects—something really good,' he said.

"Well, there was quite a lot of work to be done, so I said, 'I think we can arrange that. What else?'

"He paused again, and after a while said, 'How about this? How about we don't actually kill it, but just shelve it? If we get rich again, maybe I can go back to it.'

"That was a concession that cost me nothing, and I always agree to those. 'Okay. What else?' Keep asking until you know everything the other person wants—sometimes the third or fourth request is the key. You may not be able to give him everything—or it may not be desirable to do so—but it doesn't hurt to ask.

"And finally he shook his head and said, 'You know, I'm really surprised I got away with it this long. I'd just hoped I could get it finished before the inevitable happened. You just beat my timetable, that's all.' People frequently understand the issue; they just don't think it's in their best interests to seem to understand.

"'I did some really good design work on this project—I think a few things can be salvaged into other work,' he said. And that was the best outcome of all."

Günter's process is important. Respect and deal with the emotions that people have about the work and about change and give them a chance to participate in the negotiation, and you may accomplish two goals: better quality of work, and an employee who reinvests in the organization.

"It was worth it, because at the end, I had a team player again," Günter concluded.

Conflict between project driver and portfolio driver. There can be a conflict between the driving constraint of a single project and the driver of multiple projects. For example, the overall concern may be revenue generation, but for an individual project, time may trump. Be aware of how different constraints shape decisions, and be prepared to balance drivers among projects to achieve optimum results.

Optimization of the whole may require suboptimization of the parts. When your concern is total value or total return on a portfolio of projects, it doesn't necessarily follow that you should adopt a strategy of maximizing the return on each individual project. A 100 percent improvement on a $200,000 project is worth less than a 20 percent improvement on a $2,000,000 project.

Resource allocation is the ultimate priority tool. The Federal Reserve basically has one tool, the adjustment of a key interest rate, with which to manage the economy. Moving it up and down has ripple effects that, while not completely controllable, have some predictive and causative value. Similarly, when you are managing multiple projects, there is only one core tool: the allocation of resources. How, where, and when you allocate resources to projects drives all other decisions, because inherently there's always more useful work that could be done than there are resources available with which to do it. Any priority decision not backed by a resource-allocation strategy is simply hot air; people will quickly realize that where the resources are, there also is the priority.

Different projects have different stakeholders. As an individual project manager, you quickly learn the value of having a project champion—someone with political power and influence who's on your side. When you are managing multiple projects, you become the enemy to at least some of your own project managers and customers. Your project managers and key stakeholders will ally in a project manager/project champion role, limiting your authority and causing you to reverse at least some of the resource decisions that you make. Part of the solution to this problem is learning in advance what fights you are going to lose, and not fighting them. Project managers at any level are hired hands, and we are here to serve the needs of our customers. Therefore, our decision-making authority is not absolute, and tends to be exercised in conjunction and coordination with other power centers in our project environment.

Importance and interest are not the same. The degree of technological challenge and creativity required by a project is not necessarily proportional to the value that can be received. This may mean reluctance on the part of some members of your technical team to take roles on less interesting projects. It may mean a tendency on the part of some members of the team to add a level of technological interest to a project that doesn't necessarily require it—or whose value can be diminished thereby. Keep an eye out for these tendencies, allocating projects to top team members not only by organizational importance but also by interest and challenge. Share the fun.

Notes

1. Of course, the real motive for the extra horsepower, besides bragging rights, has to do with the ability to play games and watch DVDs on long transcontinental flights … which is toy value as well.
2. For more, see Dobson, Michael S., 1999b, 90–92.

Conclusion

The cartoon character Superchicken (he appeared on *George of the Jungle*), had a motto: "You knew the job was dangerous when you took it."

The goal of this book is to help you see both the immense rewards and satisfaction that you can gain from effective technical leadership, as well as the minefield beneath your feet. While it's always nerve-racking to stand in a minefield, if you have a good map and the mines are clearly marked, it's really not as dangerous as it looks.

Using the inside/out management model, you focused first on yourself: your goals, skills, vision, values, style, needs, attitudes, and personal integrity and commitment. You are your own primary tool, and self-development and growth are the best assets that you have.

Surrounding the core are the four areas in which you can develop your management ability: 1) techniques of motivation, project management, finance, hiring and firing; 2) tools of knowledge, resources, and power; 3) communications skills both logical and emotional; and 4) systems, from total quality management to business process reengineering and beyond.

Unlike certain physical disciplines, management and people skills are the subject of lifelong learning. Take today's step and then tomorrow's step, and you'll be on the path to achievement. By completing the personal action plan in Exercise 20, you'll have a good idea what to do next.

Exercise 20

My Personal Action Plan

Take a few minutes to go back over the sections of this book, noting those areas you've found to be of particular concern or value in your situation. Select no more than three areas to start; you can always add more later.

1. My top three areas for action are:

   _____
   _____
   _____

2. For each idea, this is my personal commitment to taking action:

   _____
   _____
   _____

A. Area for Improvement:

_____

Action Steps for This Area:

_____
_____
_____
_____
_____

B. Area for Improvement:

_____

Action Steps for This Area:

_____
_____
_____
_____
_____

C. Area for Improvement:

_____

Action Steps for This Area:

_____
_____
_____
_____
_____

Bibliography

Adams, Scott. 1996. *The Dilbert Principle*. New York: HarperBusiness.

Alessandra, Tony. 1997. *Mastering Your Message* (audiotape). Mission Kansas: SkillPath Publications.

Benford, Gregory. 1997. *Foundation's Fear*. New York: HarperPrism.

Berkowitz, Ralph, Ph.D. 1994. *Moving to the Next Generation of Quality: Achieving World Class Status*. Nashville, Tennessee: Luton Printing.

Blanchard, Kenneth, Ph.D., Donald Carew, Ed.D., and Eunice Parisi-Carew, Ed.D. 1990. *The One Minute Manager Builds High Performing Teams*. New York: William Morrow & Company.

Boyett, Joseph H., and Henry P. Conn. 1992. *Workforce 2000: The Revolution Reshaping American Business*. New York: Plume.

Bramson, Robert. 1986. Coping With Difficult People. *What the Pros Say About Success* (audiotape). New York: American Management Association/Simon & Schuster Audio Division.

Branwyn, Gareth. 1997. Jargon Watch, in Binary Beat: Generica, Semisweet Land of Jitterati, by James Coates. *Chicago Tribune* (Sunday, June 8): Section 5, p. 5.

Brassard, Michael, and Diane Ritter. 1994. *The Memory Jogger™ II: A Pocket Guide of Tools for Continuous Improvement and Effective Planning*, 1st ed. Methuen, Massachusetts: GOAL/QPC.

Brown, Jerry, and Denise Dudley. 1989. *The Supervisor's Guide*. Mission, Kansas: SkillPath Publications.

Caroselli, Marlene, Ed.D. 1993. *Hiring and Firing: What Every Manager Needs to Know*, rev. ed. Mission, Kansas: SkillPath Publications.

Carr, David K., and Henry J. Johansson. 1995. *Best Practices in Reengineering: What Works and What Doesn't in the Reengineering Process*. New York: McGraw-Hill.

Carr-Ruffino, Norma. 1993. *The Promotable Woman: Advancing Through Leadership Skills*, 2d ed. Belmont, California: Wadsworth Publishing Company.

Carroll, Lewis. 1960. *The Annotated Alice*. New York: Clarkson N. Potter.

Clarke, Arthur C. 1999. *Greetings, Carbon-Based Bipeds!: Collected Essays 1934–1998*. New York: St. Martin's Press.

Covey, Stephen R. 1989. *The Seven Habits of Highly Effective People*. New York: Simon and Schuster.

Crittenden, Ann. 1994. Trendicators: Where *Workforce 2000* Went Wrong. *Working Women* (August): 18.

Crosby, Philip B. 1980. *Quality Is Free*. New York: Mentor Books.

Dobson, Michael S. 1996. *Practical Project Management*. Mission, Kansas: SkillPath Publications.

———. 1999a. *Exploring Personality Styles*. Mission, Kansas: SkillPath Publications.

———. 1999b. *The Juggler's Guide to Managing Multiple Projects*. Newtown Square, Pennsylvania: Project Management Institute.

Dobson, Michael Singer, and Deborah Singer Dobson. 1997. *Coping With Supervisory Nightmares*. Mission, Kansas: SkillPath Publications.

———. 2000. *Managing UP!* New York: AMACOM.

Dobyns, Lloyd, and Clare Crawford-Mason. 1991. *Quality or Else: The Revolution in World Business*. Boston: Houghton Mifflin.

Drucker, Peter F. 1973. *Management: Tasks, Responsibilities, Practices*. New York: Harper & Row.

Elgin, Suzette Haden. 1989. *Success With the Gentle Art of Verbal Self-Defense*. Englewood Cliffs, New Jersey: Prentice-Hall.

Fielder, Barbara. 1996. *Motivation in the Workplace*. Mission, Kansas: SkillPath Publications.

Filipczak, Bob. 1994. It's Just a Job: Generation X at Work. *Training* (April): 20–27.

Finkler, Steven A., Ph.D., C.P.A. 1983. *The Complete Guide to Finance & Accounting for Nonfinancial Managers*. Englewood Cliffs, New Jersey: Prentice Hall.

Fisher, Roger, and William Ury. 1981. *Getting to Yes: Negotiating Agreement Without Giving In*. New York: Penguin Books.

Freeman, Lawrence H., Ph.D., and Terry R. Bacon, Ph.D. 1990. *Shipley Associates Style Guide*, rev. ed. Bountiful, Utah: Shipley Associates.

Friedman, Paul. 1991. *How to Deal With Difficult People*. Mission, Kansas: SkillPath Publications.

Fuller, George. 1995. *The First-Time Supervisor's Survival Guide*. Englewood Cliffs, New Jersey: Prentice Hall.

Goleman, Daniel. 1995. *Emotional Intelligence*. New York: Bantam Books.

Hammer, Michael, and James Champy. 1993. *Reengineering the Corporation*. New York: HarperBusiness.

Heinlein, Robert. 1963. *Glory Road*. New York: G. P. Putnam's Sons.

———. 1968. *The Moon Is a Harsh Mistress*. New York: Berkley Medallion.

Herzberg, Frederick, et al. 1959. *The Motivation to Work*. New York: Wiley & Sons.

Humphrey, Watts S. 1997. *Managing Technical People: Innovation, Teamwork, and the Software Process*. Reading, Massachusetts: Addison-Wesley.

Hutchins, Greg. 1993. *ISO 9000: A Comprehensive Guide to Registration, Audit Guidelines, and Successful Certification*. Essex Junction, Vermont: Oliver Wight Publications.

Imai, Masaaki. 1986. *Kaizen: The Key to Japan's Competitive Success*. New York: McGraw-Hill.

Keirsey, David, and Marilyn Bates. 1984. *Please Understand Me: Character and Temperament Types*. Del Mar, California: Prometheus Nemesis Book Company.

Kerzner, Harold, Ph.D. 1998. *Project Management A Systems Approach to Planning, Scheduling, and Controlling*, 6th ed. New York: John Wiley and Sons.

Kormanski, Chuck, Ed.D., and Andrew Mozenter. 1987. A New Model of Team Building: A Technology for Today and Tomorrow. *The 1987 Annual: Developing Human Resources*. San Diego: University Associates, 255–68.

Korzybski, Alfred. 1958. *Science and Sanity: An Introduction to Non-Aristotelian Systems and General Semantics*, 5th ed. Englewood, New Jersey: Institute of General Semantics.

Kotler, Philip. 1984. *Marketing Management: Analysis, Planning, and Control*, 5th ed. New Jersey: Prentice-Hall, Inc.

Kutchner, Ronald. 1988. Economic and Employment Projections to 2000: Overview and Implications. *Projections 2000: Bulletin 2302*. Washington, D.C.: U.S. Department of Labor, Bureau of Labor Statistics (March).

Machiavelli, Niccoló, 1908. *The Prince*. London: Everyman Library.

Main, Jeremy. 1994. *Quality Wars: The Triumphs and Defeats of American Business (A Juran Institute Report)*. New York: The Free Press.

Maslow, Abraham H. 1954. *Motivation and Personality*. New York: Harper & Row.

Nelson, Bob. 1996. Dump the Cash, Load on the Praise. *Personnel Journal* (July): 65–70.

Niven, Larry, and Jerry Pournelle. 1974. *The Mote in God's Eye*. New York: Simon & Schuster.

Ouchi, William G. 1981. *Theory Z*. New York: Addison-Wesley.

Pachter, Barbara, and Marjorie Brody. 1995. *Climbing the Corporate Ladder: What You Need to Know and Do to Be a Promotable Person*. Mission, Kansas: SkillPath Publications.

Peters, Thomas J., and Brian Tracy. 1989. *The Management Advantage* (audiotape). Chicago: Nightingale-Conant.

———, and Robert H. Waterman Jr. 1982. *In Search of Excellence: Lessons from America's Best-Run Companies*. New York: Warner Books.

Satir, Virginia. 1988. *The New Peoplemaking*. Mountain View, California: Science and Behavior Books.

Seligman, Martin E. P., Ph.D. 1991. *Learned Optimism*. New York: Alfred A. Knopf.

Senge, Peter M. 1990. *The Fifth Discipline: The Art and Practice of Learning Organization*. New York: Currency Doubleday.

————, et al. 1994. *The Fifth Discipline Fieldbook: Strategies and Tools for Building a Learning Organization.* New York: Currency Doubleday.

Silverberg, Robert, ed. 1970. *The Science Fiction Hall of Fame: Volume 1.* New York: Doubleday.

Stein, Richard J. 1993. *Learning to Manage Technical Professionals: Crossing the Swamp.* Reading, Massachusetts: Addison-Wesley.

Stone, Wilfred, and J. G. Bell. 1972. *Prose Style: A Handbook for Writers,* 2d ed. New York: McGraw-Hill.

Strauss, William, and Neil Howe. 1991. *Generations: The History of America's Future 1584–2069.* New York: William Morrow.

Tannen, Deborah, Ph.D. 1990. *You Just Don't Understand: Women and Men in Conversation.* New York: Ballentine Books.

Temme, Jim. 1993. *Productivity Power: 250 Great Ideas for Being More Productive.* Mission, Kansas: SkillPath Publications.

————. 1996. *Team Power: How to Build and Grow Successful Teams.* Mission, Kansas: SkillPath Publications.

Toffler, Alvin. 1970. *Future Shock.* New York: Bantam Books.

Towers, Mark. 1993. *Dynamic Delegation: A Manager's Guide for Active Empowerment.* Mission, Kansas: SkillPath Publications.

Troutman, Kathryn, et al. 1995. *The Federal Resume Guidebook.* Washington, D.C.: The Resume Place.

Turow, Scott. 1996. *The Laws of Our Fathers.* New York: Farrar Strauss Giroux.

U.S. Department of Labor, Bureau of Labor Statistics. 1988. *Projections 2000: Bulletin 2302.* Washington, D.C.

Walton, Mary. 1986. *The Deming Management Method.* New York: Perigee Books.

Weisbord, Marvin R. 1990. *Productive Workplaces: Organizing and Managing for Dignity, Meaning, and Community.* San Francisco: Jossey-Bass Publishers.

Weldon, Michele. 1997. Working Smart: Communications Overload: Knowing When It's Wise to Stop Talking. *Chicago Tribune* (Sunday, April 20): Section 13.

Whitaker, Mark. 1997. Focus on Technology: How We Did It: Interview with Bill Gates and Steve Ballmer of Microsoft. *Newsweek* (June 23): 78–82.

Wilson, Robert Anton. 1982. *Right Where You Are Sitting Now.* Berkeley, California: And/Or Press.

Young, David. 1997. Biz Tips: Four and Out. *Chicago Tribune* (Monday, April 14): Section 4, p. 3.

Index

404 (Clueless)   102
80/20 rule   *See* Pareto Principle

A

abilities   4, 12, 14, 28, 64, 119–21, 125, 133, 137,
   142
   See also GREAT
accomplishment   18, 62, 99, 107, 153
accounting   77, 89, 111, 143
achievement   1, 7, 11, 20, 72, 105, 119, 128, 131,
   141, 165
action plan   1, 5, 7, 15–16, 21, 24, 165
action steps   21–25, 32, 166
adjourning stage   119
adminisphere   102
administration   35, 94
advancement   15, 23, 27, 72, 141–42
Affirmative Action   66, 76
alternatives   11, 29
American National Standards Institute   84
Americans with Disabilities Act   76
anger   52, 55, 118
appeasement engineer   102
aptitudes   4, 74
architects   3
asocial behavior   73
assessment   68, 133–34
assets   33, 77 78, 165
attention span   138
attitude   9–10, 14, 20, 27, 43, 53, 68, 77, 105, 120,
   143–44, 153, 159
   problem   136
authoritarian   *See* Theory X
authority   9–10, 14–15, 17, 21–22, 31, 37–40, 43, 52,
   62, 75, 82, 86, 88–89, 107, 117, 122–23, 125,
   127–28, 130, 134, 140–42, 144, 164
autonomy   85–86, 139

B

BATNA   *See* best alternative to a negotiated agreement
   (BATNA)
BPR   *See* business process engineering (BPR)
behavior modification   37, 69
behaviors   *See* organizational, behaviors

behavioral   45, 52–53, 67–68, 75–76, 107, 113, 136
below-average performers   12
benchmarks   87
best alternative to a negotiated agreement (BATNA)   133
betamaxed   102
biomedical research   20
bit diddlers   102
body language   53, 55
brainstorm (ing)   91, 116, 119, 147
breakeven   12
buddy system   116
budget(s)   4, 37, 39, 77–78, 94, 128, 147–48, 153,
   157
bureaucracy   142, 151
bureaucratic organization   88
business case   65, 115
business process reengineering (BPR)   83–84, 94, 106,
   115, 165

C

CIT   *See* continuous improvement, team(s) (CIT)
caffeine   73, 102
   See also coffee, java, *and* Jolt
can't-do issue   72, 76
can't-do problem   69, 74
career   14, 25, 33, 64, 78, 82, 129, 142, 159
   -limiting moves   95
   change   3, 27, 35, 80
   decision   4
   goal(s)   5, 9, 35, 137
   opportunities   19, 23
   planning   49
   satisfaction   3
   strategy   5
cause and effect diagram   *See* Ishikawa diagram
chainsaw consultants   102
challenge   15–16, 20, 49, 63, 70, 72, 75, 86, 90, 99,
   105, 115, 136, 138–39, 147, 153–54, 156, 161,
   164
change order   147
change resistance   105
checkpoints   62
chip jewelry   102
circling the drain   102
civil service   14

coaching   42, 62–64, 76, 116, 124
   style   *See* S2 (coaching style)
code pie   102
coffee   102
   See also java
commitment   4, 28, 41–42, 82, 84–85, 87–88, 92, 94,
   96–97, 105, 118, 120, 140, 165
communication(s)   13, 31, 37, 49–51, 53–54, 57–59,
   62, 68–69, 71, 76, 88, 93, 101, 117, 120–21,
   124, 129–30, 165
   one-way   55
company policies   *See* policy(ies), company
competence   4–5, 12
competitive advantage   82
competitive position   84
computer programmers   15
confidential information   64
conflict   64, 73–76, 88, 99, 101, 107, 117–20, 124,
   134, 142, 147, 151–52, 161, 164
   management   37, 74, 119
   resolution   49, 118, 120
conformance to requirements   13, 93, 161
connotation   51–54, 136
consensus   118–20, 122, 152, 161
continuing education   12
continuous improvement   90–91
   team(s) (CIT)   89
contracts   39
   union   74
control   1, 19, 22, 29, 39–41, 49, 61–62, 78, 82, 99,
   123, 125, 127, 130, 136, 142, 153, 156, 159,
   161
   See also POSDIC
   chart   89, 91
      See also process control chart
coordination   61, 164
core business processes   84
corporate   11, 13, 45, 92, 99, 103
   culture   49, 101, 103, 114
   environment   11
   loyalty   138
   mission   22
cost cutting   84
cost of quality   *See* quality, cost of
creativity   41, 117, 161, 164
credibility   52, 58, 73, 95
criticism   12, 68, 76, 83, 87, 94, 138
cross-training   89, 111, 115–16, 124, 135
cube farm   102
cultural diversity   93
culture   41, 86, 99, 101, 103–04, 119
   See also corporate, culture; cultural diversity; *and*
      organizational, culture
customer   12–14, 64, 84–85, 87, 90–91, 104, 121,
   123, 133, 141, 143–45, 147–48, 152–53,
   158–61, 164
   -centered   10, 13, 159, 161
   -focus(ed)   59, 105–08
   focus(ed)   10, 70, 90, 92, 101, 106–08
      See also total quality management (TQM)
cybernetic model   83

D
dawn patrol   102
deadline(s)   62–63, 70–71, 115–16, 122, 153, 156
decision(s)   8, 10–14, 18, 20, 22–23, 29, 39–41, 53,
   62, 65, 71, 75–76, 87–88, 91, 95, 107, 109, 115,
   121, 156
      process   12, 58
decision-making   117, 119, 127, 130, 164
delegate   11, 23, 61, 63–64, 122, 156
delegatee   63–64
delegating style   *See* S4 (delegating style)
delegation   24, 37, 61–64, 117
Deming Cycle   90
democratic   *See* Theory Y
de-motivation   140
denotation   51
design   30, 35, 62, 74, 80, 152, 154, 162, 163
   professionals   3
desire   4, 11, 59, 64, 123, 133, 144, 159–60
developmental   42, 51, 137
   assignments   21, 23, 63
   conference   76
   level   42
difficult people   135–36
digerati   102
Dilbert   3, 13
   Principle   17
directing   35, 42
   style   *See* S1 (directing style)
discipline   73–74, 122, 125, 149
dislike   10, 19, 41, 51, 64, 75
dissatisfiers   71
distrust   51, 62, 143
diversity   28
   See also cultural diversity
don't-know problem   69, 74
downsizing   69, 75, 95
dress code   13, 67, 135

E
educational background   3
EEO/Affirmative Action   *See* Affirmative Action
ego   13
email   52–53, 160
emotion(s)   8–9, 12, 52–53, 76, 103, 162–63
   See also emotional
emotional   4, 11, 27, 61, 123, 136, 165
   See also emotion(s) *and* interpersonal and emotional
      strategies
   challenges   20
   content   53
   intelligence   13
   reactions   12
   whiplash   3
empowerment   41, 85–86, 88–89, 115, 117, 120,
   128, 139
engineers   3, 59, 89, 94, 111, 117, 127, 162

entrepreneurship   85
equipment   37, 65, 67, 69, 88, 102, 120, 135, 138
European Community   85
evaluation   30, 49, 67–68, 78, 154
executive management   103, 125
executive perspective   14, 78
expectations   10, 90, 108, 120–21, 151, 161
    See also GREAT
"extraverts"   10
extrovert   10
eye contact   55, 66

F

factual thinking   3
fear   64, 87, 93, 95, 102, 127, 138
federal agencies   94
federal government   14
feedback   22–23, 43, 54, 58, 62, 64, 67, 71, 76, 113,
    116, 135, 138, 140, 161
feudalism   88
finance   10, 70, 77, 92, 165
financial statements   77
fire in the belly   4
firing   49, 165
fishbone diagram   See Ishikawa diagram
flow chart   91
focus   3, 20–21, 25, 27, 30, 49, 52, 66, 73, 75,
    84–87, 89, 94, 104, 113–16, 119, 121, 134, 137,
    140, 153–54, 161
    See also customer, -centered; customer, -focus(ed);
        and customer, focus(ed)
    group   114–15
    team   99, 117, 158
forecast   77
forming stage   118

G

GREAT (Great/Roles/Expectations/Abilities/Time)   121
Gantt chart   122
geekosphere   102
geeks   3, 135
geeksploitation   102
Generation X(ers)   133, 138–39
goal-oriented   59
goal oriented   52, 109
goal-related   25
goal statement   157
Godzilla Principle   30
good-enough point   12
goodies   114
grammar and usage   51–52
group norm   73
growth   21, 23, 46, 49, 67, 79, 83, 87, 105, 113, 125,
    137, 140, 165
guidance   61, 63, 75

H

hard-skill training   See training, hard-skill
hero syndrome   64
Herzberg's motivation model   71
hierarchical   49, 87
hierarchy   37, 69, 72, 123, 125, 134, 153
hiring   49, 65–66, 125, 165
histogram   91
human interaction   9
human resources   See resources, human
hygiene factors   71

I

IDP   See individual development plan (IDP)
IQ   12, 52
ISO-9000   81, 84–85
    See also registrar (for ISO-9000)
ISO-9001   84
ISO-9002   84
ISO-9003   84
ISO-9004   84
"I can do it better myself" syndrome   63
immigrants   92
impatience   64
inappropriate work behaviors   118
    See also behavior modification
inclusion   22–23, 71
independent work   8, 11
individual development plan (IDP)   113, 115, 128
industrial model   83
industrial revolution   81, 151–52
inertia   22, 94, 105
informal information channels   142
information technology   3, 11, 83–84, 101, 142
innovation   59, 87, 117, 125–28, 139
insecurity   62, 64
inside/out management model   165
internal spy network   145
International Organization for Standardization   84
interpersonal   14, 121
    and emotional strategies   12
    skill(s)   66, 121
    transactions   14
interview   65–66, 125
introvert(s)   10
Intuitive Thinker (NT)   14
    See also visionary, leader
Ishikawa diagram   86, 91

J

Japanese   30, 86, 89–90
    management style   41
        See also Kaizen and kanban
java   102
    See also coffee

jerk filter   54
jitterati   102
job   11, 14–15, 18, 20, 24, 27–29, 42–43, 46, 58, 62, 65–69, 73–78, 88, 109–10, 116–17, 120, 122, 127, 130–31, 133–34, 140–42, 156, 161
   See also training, on-the-job
   and Generation X   138–39
   assignment(s)   64, 70, 113–14
   description(s)   25, 65–66, 120
   performance   73–74
   satisfaction   18, 71–72
   satisfier   8, 72
Jolt   102
Juran Institute   83
just-in-time inventory management   86

K

Kaizen   86, 89
   See also total quality management (TQM)
kanban   86
   See also just-in-time inventory management
knowledge   8, 12–15, 42, 53, 68, 78–80, 82, 99, 105, 107–08, 116, 120–22, 127, 130–31, 137, 154–56, 159, 165

L

language   51, 53, 75–77, 84, 136, 157
leadership   1, 3–4, 7, 9–10, 13–15, 17, 20–22, 27, 30, 41, 43, 49–50, 61, 69, 93, 95, 117, 119–21, 125–27, 138, 143, 149, 154, 160, 165
learning organization   86
lifelong learning   82, 137, 165
line department(s)   101, 142–43
listening   55, 62, 132, 139
logic   8–9, 12, 76, 103
long-range planning   See planning, long-range

M

MBE   See management by exception (MBE)
MBO   See management by objectives (MBO)
MBWA   See management by wandering/walking around (MBWA)
MIL-Q 9858A   85
maintenance   125–27
management as a catalyst   88
management as a maintenance activity   125
management as an occupation   17
management by exception (MBE)   86
management by objectives (MBO)   81, 86–87
management by wandering/walking around (MBWA)   81, 88, 94–95
management initiatives   94, 96, 106
management systems   71, 87, 94, 156
market share   83, 87

marketing   10, 13, 35, 77, 111, 117
   -driven company   101
Maslow's Hierarchy of Needs   69, 134
master skill list   124
matrix   49
   organization   85
McKinsey 7-S Framework   49–50
medical professionals   3
medicine   27
meetings   18, 22, 40, 73, 103, 116, 118, 120
metamessage   59
micromanagement   64
middle management   127
minorities   92
mission   11, 14, 28, 37, 70, 87, 90, 101, 107, 118–20, 124
   creep   145, 147
   statement(s)   28, 37, 87
momentum   94
money   19, 21, 23, 29, 67–68, 73, 120, 128, 134, 143, 162
monitor pets   102
morale   41–42, 49, 62, 87, 115, 120, 139–40
motivation   37, 49, 62, 68–69, 71–73, 134, 139–40, 165
   self-   42
motivational techniques   138
motivators   71–72, 134
multiple project environment   115, 161
mushroom syndrome   58
Myers-Briggs Type Indicator   10, 14
   See also Intuitive Thinker (NT) and visionary, leader

N

NT   See Intuitive Thinker and visionary, leader
negativity   11, 15, 118
negotiation   49, 64, 120, 130, 132–33, 136, 162–63
   principled   118
networking   23, 111, 129–30
nonlogical thinking   9
norming stage   119

O

OPD   See obnoxious personality disorder (OPD)
obedience   22
objectives   41, 68, 86–87, 94, 117, 120, 145, 152, 157–58
   See also organizational, objectives
obnoxious personality disorder (OPD)   135
occupational safety and health   76
office politics   See politics, office
on-the-job training   See training, on-the-job
one-way communication   See communication(s), one-way
open-door policies   See policy(ies), open-door
optimists   20

organizational   11, 15, 37, 41, 64–65, 76, 80, 86–88, 90, 104, 113, 120–21, 139, 149, 160, 164
  behaviors   95
  change   101, 106–08
    model   105
  culture   46, 101, 105–06, 108, 128
  decision   9
  development   28, 49, 119
  dynamics   101
  fluidity   88
  goal(s)   14, 78, 129
  issues   18, 29
  objectives   127
  perspective   9
  problems   50, 68
  restrictions   18
  structure   84, 96, 128
output   5, 73, 89, 119, 127, 154
overloading   113, 115
oversight   61
oversupervising   140
overtime   20, 70, 156
overwork   115

P

PDCA   *See* plan, do, check act (PDCA)
PDSA   *See* plan, do, study, act (PDSA)
PEBCAK   *See* "problem exists between chair and keyboard"
PERT chart   122
POSDIC (Plan/Organize/Staff/Direct/Inspect/Control)   61
paradigm(s)   12, 20, 82–83, 151–52
paraphrasing   54–55
parenting   139
Pareto Chart   91
Pareto Principle   25, 91, 133
patronization   64
people-centered   41–43, 46
people skills   8, 10, 49, 120, 122, 124, 165
perception   52–53, 69
perfectionism   11, 24, 62, 64
  See also unyielding perfectionist
performance   28, 30, 42, 45, 62, 64, 68, 74–76, 87, 113, 115, 118–21, 129, 133, 140, 142, 147, 152–53, 156–57, 161
  appraisal(s)   65, 67, 71
  indicators   116
  issues   75, 136
  measurement   93
  standard(s)   70, 86, 93, 121
performing stage   119
personal   4
  characteristics   9
  growth   86, 153
  power   129, 132
  problems   139

personality   7, 9, 23, 32, 41, 82, 124, 134
  See also Myers-Briggs Type Indicator *and* obnoxious personality disorder
  struggles   76
  traits   66
persuasive   43, 53
pessimists   20
Peter Principle   4
pizza   73, 102
plan(s)   5, 23, 25, 49, 73, 85, 87, 90, 113, 119
  See also action plan; POSDIC; plan, do, check, act (PDCA); *and* plan, do, study, act (PDSA)
plan, do, check, act (PDCA)   90
plan, do, study, act (PDSA)   89–90
planning   30, 37, 61, 78, 80, 87, 97, 106, 108, 120, 122, 142, 149, 156, 158
  See also quality, planning
  long-range   64, 127
Platinum Rule   41
policy(ies)   62, 65–66, 76, 87, 118, 125, 142
  company   72
  open-door   88
political correctness   51
political skills   145
politics   3, 40, 142
  office   8, 10, 18, 120, 141
poor management practice   138
positive thinking   20
power dynamic   129, 132
power role(s)   129–31
practice   24, 35, 58, 70, 80, 83, 86, 88, 93–95
praise   13, 71, 108, 134, 137
principled negotiation   *See* negotiation, principled
priorities   14, 25, 63–64, 153
"problem exists between chair and keyboard" (PEBCAK)   102
problem-solving   69, 131
problem solving   11, 28, 37, 90, 119, 131, 136
  structured   65
process control chart   85
procrastination   140
product champions   127
product development   84, 101, 162
  new   111, 142
productivity   1, 14–15, 41, 64, 68, 85, 88, 103–04, 107, 113, 115–16, 119–20
professional dress   13
professional skill(s)   19, 23–24
profit sharing   107
profitability   87
project   5
  See also multiple project environment
  change   147
  manager   30, 37, 122, 152, 155–56, 158–60, 164
    working   61
  oriented   3, 109, 111
  team   *See* team, project
promotion(s)   3, 27, 37, 61, 63–64, 73, 113

Q

Q101 (Ford's)   85
quality   8–13, 28, 52, 65, 70, 75, 82, 87, 89–93, 104–05, 113, 120, 125–26, 131, 143, 153, 160, 163
   See also customer, -centered quality
   assurance   49, 84, 89
   circles   89
   control   89, 92
      See also statistical quality control
   cost of   93
   improvement   83, 86, 92, 119
   management   84, 86, 92
      See also total quality management (TQM)
   movement   90–91
   planning   92
   program   85–86

R

R&D   92, 125, 143, 154
rapport   12
rationality   9, 12
recognition   62, 71–72, 86, 119, 134
recruiting   65–67
recruitment   37, 135
reengineering   81, 83–84, 115, 125
   See also business process reengineering (BPR)
registrar (for ISO-9000)   85
relationship(s)   8, 10, 13–14, 21–23, 49, 54, 65, 72, 76, 86, 91, 101, 104, 106–07, 116, 118–19, 125, 127–32, 136, 141–43, 160
   power   130–32
reorganization   95
reporting   49, 94, 122
requirements   53, 65–66, 84, 148, 153
   See also conformance to requirements
research   42, 65, 67, 71, 82, 89, 108, 127, 145
   See also biomedical research
resources   12, 16, 37, 39, 62, 80, 84, 96, 119–20, 123, 130, 142–43, 153, 157–58, 164–65
   human   65–67, 74, 77, 144
respect   9–10, 14, 21–22, 37, 40, 43, 52, 64, 129, 134, 163
   power   130–31, 133, 137
rewarding   11, 21, 64, 70
rhetoric power   130, 132
risk taking   117
run chart   91

S

S1 (directing style)   42
S2 (coaching style)   42
S3 (supporting style)   42
S4 (delegating style)   42
SDWT   *See* team, work, self-directed (SDWT)

SMART (specific, measurable, agreed-upon, realistic, time-specific)   106, 122, 157
SPC   *See* statistical process control (SPC)
sales   4, 10, 87, 117, 156
Scatter Diagram   91
scheduling board   115
scientific management   81, 88, 151
Second Law of Thermodynamics   94
self-assessment   1, 5, 7, 17–19, 21, 136
self-confidence   41–42
self-directed work team (SDWT)   *See* team, work, self-directed
self-leadership   127
self-management   20, 127
self-motivation   *See* motivation, self-
semantic content   53
seminar   68, 96, 139
semi-official positions   37
senior executive service   14
senior management   40, 65, 70, 77–78, 92, 95, 107, 132, 134, 141
sensitive information   13
sexual harassment   76
shared values   49
Sharpen the Saw   12
Shewhart Cycle   90
Situational Leadership II   42, 46
skunk works   127–28
social awkwardness   15
soft-skill training   *See* training, soft-skill
software engineering   42
specialist group structure   117
specialization   14, 130, 159
staffing departments   101, 142–43
staffing development   28, 61, 64, 68, 92, 115
standards   8, 10, 12, 70, 76, 84–86, 121, 125, 157
star performers   12
statistical process control (SPC)   89
statistical quality control   89
statistics   89, 92
stereotypes   7
storming phase   118
strategic vision   *See* vision, strategic
strategy   14, 16, 30, 49, 51, 55, 68–69, 84, 114, 133, 142–43, 162, 164
structure   49, 68, 85, 88, 92, 109, 111–13, 116–17, 125, 134–36
   See also organizational, structure, *and* team, structure
structured problem solving   *See* problem, solving, structured
style   20, 37, 41–42, 46, 49, 62, 64, 66, 114, 152, 165
   See also S1 (directing style), S2 (coaching style), S3 (supporting style), *and* S4 (delegating style)
   flexibility   9, 41, 46
   supervisory   41, 43, 45–46, 49, 127

success   4–5, 7, 11–13, 15, 20, 27–28, 70, 82, 89, 94–95, 97, 117, 119–22, 142–43, 146–47, 149, 155
sugar   73, 102, 134
supervision   20, 37, 49, 78, 99, 125, 139, 153
    See also oversupervising
supervisor(s)   37–38, 45, 67, 69, 75, 88, 139, 143–44
    working   61, 64
supervisory role(s)   43, 119
supervisory style   *See* style, supervisory
supporting style   *See* S3 (supporting style)
survivor's guilt   75
systems   37, 39, 49, 84–85, 87, 89–90, 94, 116, 120, 123, 127, 165
    approach to human beings   81
    tracking and control   115

T

TQM   *See* total quality management (TQM)
tardiness   73
targets of excellence   85
task-centered   41–42, 46
team(s)   11, 14–15, 18, 24, 28, 40, 58, 64–66, 77 78, 83, 86 91, 95, 99, 101, 103 09, 111, 115–35, 139–44
    See also continuous improvement, team(s) *and* teaming
    building   49, 68, 75, 91, 121
    composition   124
    concept   75, 118
    culture   103–05, 117, 120
    development   122
    goal(s)   88–89, 117–127, 129
    leader(s)   37, 45
    learning   87
    member(s)   17, 22, 29, 37–39, 41–44, 46, 49, 51, 59, 62–64, 66–68, 71, 73, 81–82, 86, 91, 97, 105, 107–08, 113, 115–25, 129–37, 139–40, 142, 152–53, 158, 164
        See also teamwork
    performance   71, 117, 124
    player(s)   70, 82, 163
    process(es)   120–21
    project   23, 37, 89, 122–24, 127, 153, 161
    structure   99, 117–18, 120–22, 127
    tiger   127–28
    work   89, 91, 117, 122
        self-directed (SDWT)   89, 116, 126–27
teaming   91, 117, 120
    See also team(s)
teamwork   75, 87, 88, 90, 101, 116, 117, 121, 122, 140
    See also team, member(s)
technical   43, 49, 61, 101, 104, 130, 136, 145, 149, 151–55, 165
    See also training, technical
    challenges   18, 64
    issues   12, 157
problems   13
professional(s)   1, 3–4, 7, 9–15, 17–20, 27–28, 38, 52–53, 58, 62, 64–65, 67–69, 71, 73, 76, 81–82, 91, 94, 99, 107, 109, 122, 129, 133–35, 141, 154, 159–60
    as managers   14
    culture   101
    of technical   133
    skill(s)   13, 76, 105, 113, 120–21, 133–34, 137–38
    wizard(ry)   135, 138
    work   11, 27, 49, 64, 138
technoliteracy   138
technological change   83, 138
termination   73–74
Theory X   41–42, 88
Theory Y   41–42
Theory Z   41
tiger team(s)   *See* team(s), tiger
time and-motion study   88
time management   25
tone of voice   53
total quality management (TQM)   81–84, 86, 89, 90–91, 104, 106, 115, 165
    See also customer, -focus(ed), customer, focus(ed), *and* Kaizen
tracking and control system   *See* systems, tracking and control
trainers   68
training   12, 21–24, 37, 41, 49, 69, 74–76, 80, 92–93, 105, 113, 117, 119–20, 124–25, 127, 134, 139, 149
    See also cross-training
    hard-skill   68
    soft-skill   68
    on-the-job   63, 68, 120
    technical   120
transition   3–4, 7, 17, 19–20, 27, 31, 106
treeware   102
Tuckman model   118, 127
turnover   116, 133–35

U

understudy   116, 135
union contracts   *See* contracts, union
unofficial organization   129, 141
unyielding perfectionist   135
    See also perfectionism

V

value(s)   8–14, 16, 28, 45, 68, 71, 76, 80, 83, 88, 101, 107–08, 118, 120, 138, 141, 155–56, 164–65
    -driven   85
    added   11, 29
    core   4, 85
    shared   49–50
    toy   160

vision   28, 70, 87, 107, 118, 120, 134, 138, 165
    statement   101
    strategic   14
visionary   14, 44, 71
    leader   14, 71
        See also Intuitive Thinker
visual management   115, 122
vocabulary   52, 159
voice mail   53–54

W

WAW (Waiter-Actor-Webmaster)   102
WII-FM (What's in it for me?)   107
wages and benefits   72
walk-away power   133
walk the talk   95, 107
win/win   143–44
won't-do problem   69
work breakdown structure   122
work maturity   113, 115–16, 128
work organization   99
work rules   75
work team   *See team, work*
Workforce 2000   81, 92–93
working conditions   72
working project manager   *See project, manager, working*
working supervisor(s)   *See supervisor(s), working*
workload   3, 29, 115, 140
written goal(s)   147

Z

ZBB   *See zero-base budgeting (ZBB)*
zero defects   92–93
zero-base budgeting   94
zonks   114

Upgrade Your Project Management Knowledge with First-Class Publications from PMI

A GUIDE TO THE PROJECT MANAGEMENT BODY OF KNOWLEDGE (PMBOK® GUIDE) 2000 EDITION

Since the Project Management Institute last published *A Guide to the Project Management Body of Knowledge (PMBOK® Guide)* in 1996, the publication has received widespread acclaim. The *PMBOK® Guide* serves as a reference for anyone interested in project management by focusing on knowledge and practices applicable to most projects most of the time.

The *PMBOK® Guide* has become the de facto global standard for project management. And, its acceptance as an official project management standard is evidenced by its adoption by the American National Standards Institute as an American National Standard in September 1999.

With currently over 500,000 copies of the *PMBOK® Guide* in circulation, PMI has received numerous positive comments, suggestions for corrections, and recommendations for improvements. As a consequence of those inputs and the expansion of the body of knowledge, PMI volunteers, under the project leadership of Cynthia Berg, PMP, have stepped forward once again to aid the profession by preparing an updated version of the *PMBOK® Guide*.

ISBN: 1-880410-23-0 (paperback); ISBN: 1880410222 (hardcover); ISBN: 1880410257 (CD-ROM)

PMI PROJECT MANAGEMENT SALARY SURVEY 2000 EDITION

There's more to a rewarding career in project management than a paycheck. But in today's tight labor market, it's easy to wonder how your salary and compensation package compare to your colleague down the hall or even with an associate on another continent. And current, accurate information on compensation can help you make important decisions about specific project management career choices.

In this valuable new book, you'll learn about all areas of project management compensation, such as salary, bonuses, benefits, training, and retirement. You'll get an in-depth, detailed picture of compensation trends, such as total rewards packages, providing insight into the "thought-process" behind compensation today. Information found in this new book includes learning about different methods that are being used by employers to compensate and retain project managers worldwide—from the size of bonus packages and how they relate to projects to how compensation may vary based on managing multiple projects and the budget size of those projects.

ISBN: 1-880410-26-5 (paperback)

EARNED VALUE PROJECT MANAGEMENT SECOND EDITION

"Earned value" is a project management technique that is emerging as a valuable tool in the management of all projects, including and in particular software projects. In its most simple form, earned value equates to fundamental project management.

This is not a new book, but rather it is an updated book. Authors Quentin Fleming and Joel Koppelman have made some important additions.

In many cases, there will be no changes to a given section. But in other sections, the authors have made substantial revisions to what they'd described in the first edition. Fleming and Koppelman's goal remains the same with this update: describe earned value project management in its most fundamental form, for application to all projects, of any size or complexity.

Earned Value Project Management, Second Edition may be the best-written, most easily understood project management book on the market today. Project managers will welcome this fresh translation of jargon into ordinary English. The authors have mastered a unique "early-warning" signal of impending cost problems in time for the project manager to react.

ISBN: 1880410273 (paperback)

PROJECT MANAGEMENT EXPERIENCE AND KNOWLEDGE SELF-ASSESSMENT MANUAL

In 1999, PMI® completed a role delineation study for the Project Management Professional (PMP®) Certification Examination. A role delineation study identifies a profession's major performance domains (e.g., initiating the project or planning the project). It describes the tasks that are performed in each domain, and identifies the knowledge and skills that are required to complete the task.

The role delineation task statements are presented in this manual in a format that enables you to assess how your project management experiences and training/education knowledge levels prepare you to complete each of the task statements.

Individuals may use all of these tools to enhance understanding and application of PM knowledge to satisfy personal and professional career objectives. The self-assessment rating should not be used to predict, guarantee, or infer success or failure by individuals in their project management career, examinations, or related activities.

ISBN: 1-880410-24-9, (paperback)

PROJECT MANAGEMENT PROFESSIONAL (PMP) ROLE DELINEATION STUDY

In 1999, PMI® completed a role delineation study for the Project Management Professional (PMP®) Certification Examination. In addition to being used to establish the test specifications for the examination, the study describes the tasks (competencies) PMPs perform and the project management knowledge and skills PMPs use to complete each task. Each of the study's Tasks is linked to a performance domain (e.g., Planning the Project). Each task has three components to it: what the task is, why the task is performed, and how the is task completed.

The *Role Delineation Study* is an excellent resource for educators, trainers, administrators, practitioners, and individuals interested in pursuing PMP certification.

ISBN: 1-880410-29-X, (paperback)

PM 101
ACCORDING TO THE OLDE CURMUDGEON

Former editor-in-chief for PMI®, Francis M. Webster Jr. refers to himself as "the olde curmudgeon." After reading his new book, it is difficult to see how this description applies. What Webster delivers in *PM 101 According to the Olde Curmudgeon: An Introduction to the Basic Concepts of Project Management* is insider information dispensed with a friendly arm-around-the-shoulders approach.

This is a book of veteran do's and don'ts, generously shared with novice project managers. Webster's passion is modern project management, those aspects of the field not given adequate attention in the past. You'll learn the nine essential skills of modern project management, making this an essential book for your project management library.

Writing as the "olde curmudgeon," Webster lets new project managers in on the tricks of the trade. By following his advice, the most inexperienced novice should look good. In *PM 101*, Webster shares his well-reasoned, well-organized observations. This carefully written manual is full of ideas, distinctions, rules, and metaphors—even commandments. *PM 101* is essential for new project managers who need to come off the blocks on the right foot fast!

ISBN: 1-880410-55-9, (paperback)

THE PROJECT SPONSOR GUIDE

This to-the-point and quick reading for today's busy executives and managers is a one-of-a-kind source that describes the unique and challenging support that executives and managers must provide to be effective sponsors of project teams. *The Project Sponsor Guide* is intended for executives and middle managers who will be, or are, sponsors of a project, particularly cross-functional projects. It is also helpful reading for facilitators and project leaders.

ISBN: 1-880410-15-X (paperback)

DON'T PARK YOUR BRAIN OUTSIDE
A PRACTICAL GUIDE TO IMPROVING SHAREHOLDER VALUE WITH SMART MANAGEMENT

Don't Park Your Brain Outside is the thinking person's guide to extraordinary project performance. Francis Hartman has assembled a cohesive and balanced approach to highly effective project management. It is deceptively simple. Called SMART™, this new approach is **S**trategically **M**anaged, **A**ligned, **R**egenerative, and **T**ransitional. It is based on research and best practices, tempered by hard-won experience. SMART has saved significant time and money on the hundreds of large and small, simple and complex projects on which it has been tested. Are your projects SMART? Find out by reading this people-oriented project management book with an attitude!

ISBN: 1-880410-48-6 (paperback)

THE ENTER*PRIZE* ORGANIZATION
ORGANIZING SOFTWARE PROJECTS FOR ACCOUNTABILITY AND SUCCESS

Every day project leaders are approached with haunting questions like: *What is the primary reason why projects fail? How technical should managers be? What are the duties of a project management office?* These haunting questions, along with many more, are just a few of the questions and answers Whitten discusses in his latest book, *The EnterPrize Organization*. This book is for seasoned employees, as well as for those just entering the workforce. From beginning to end, you will recognize familiar ways to define the key project roles and responsibilities, and discover some new ideas in organizing a software project.

ISBN: 1-880410-79-6 (paperback)

A FRAMEWORK FOR PROJECT MANAGEMENT

This complete project management seminar course provides experience project managers with an easy-to-use set of educational tools to help the deliver a seminar on basic project management concepts, tools, ar techniques. *A Framework for Project Management* was developed ar designed for seminar leaders by a team of experts within the PMI membership, and reviewed extensively during its development and pilotir stage by a team of PMPs.

ISBN: 1-880410-82-6 (Facilitator's Manual Set)
ISBN: 1-880410-80-X (Participants' Manual Set)

THE PMI PROJECT MANAGEMENT FACT BOOK

A comprehensive resource of information about PMI® and the professic it serves. Professionals working in project management requir information and resources to function in today's global busine: environment. Knowledge along with data collection and interpretation ar often key to determining success in the marketplace. The Proje Management Institute (PMI®) anticipates the needs of the profession wi *The PMI Project Management Fact Book*.

ISBN: 1-880410-62-1 (paperback)

PROJECT MANAGEMENT SOFTWARE SURVEY

The PMI® *Project Management Software Survey* offers an efficient way compare and contrast the capabilities of a wide variety of proje management tools. More than two hundred software tools are listed wi comprehensive information on systems features; how they perform tir analysis, resource analysis, cost analysis, performance analysis, and co reporting; and how they handle multiple projects, project trackin charting, and much more. The survey is a valuable tool to help narrow th field when selecting the best project management tools.

ISBN: 1-880410-52-4 (paperback)
ISBN: 1-880410-59-1 (CD-ROM)

THE JUGGLER'S GUIDE TO MANAGING MULTIPLE PROJECTS

This comprehensive book introduces and explains task-oriente independent, and interdependent levels of project portfolios. It says that yo must first have a strong foundation in time management and priority settin then introduces the concept of Portfolio Management to timeline multip projects, determine their resource requirements, and handle emergencie putting you in charge for possibly the first time in your life!

ISBN: 1-880410-65-6 (paperback)

RECIPES FOR PROJECT SUCCESS

This book is destined to become "the" reference book for beginnir project managers, particularly those who like to cook! Practical, logical developed project management concepts are offered in easily understoo terms in a lighthearted manner. They are applied to the everyday task cooking—from simple, single dishes, such as homemade tomato sauce fc pasta, made from the bottom up, to increasingly complex dishes or mea for groups that in turn require an understanding of more complex proje management terms and techniques. The transition between cooking an project management discussions is smooth, and tidbits of informatio provided with the recipes are interesting and humorous.

ISBN: 1-880410-58-3 (paperback)

TOOLS AND TIPS FOR TODAY'S PROJECT MANAGER

This guidebook is valuable for understanding project management and performing to quality standards. Includes project management concepts and terms—old and new—that are not only defined but also are explained in much greater detail than you would find in a typical glossary. Also included are tips on handling such seemingly simple everyday tasks as how to say "No" and how to avoid telephone tag. It's a reference you'll want to keep close at hand.
ISBN: 1-880410-61-3 (paperback)

THE FUTURE OF PROJECT MANAGEMENT

The project management profession is going through tremendous change—both evolutionary and revolutionary. Some of these changes are internally driven, while many are externally driven. Here, for the first time, is a composite view of some major trends occurring throughout the world and the implication of them on the profession of project management and on the Project Management Institute. Read the views of the 1998 PMI Research Program Team, a well-respected futurist firm, and other authors. This book represents the beginning of a journey and, through inputs from leaders and others, it will continue as a work in progress.
ISBN: 1-880410-71-0 (paperback)

NEW RESOURCES FOR PMP CANDIDATES

The following publications are resources that certification candidates can use to gain information on project management theory, principles, techniques, and procedures.

PMP RESOURCE PACKAGE

Doing Business Internationally: The Guide to Cross-Cultural Success
by Terence Brake, Danielle Walker and Thomas Walker

Earned Value Project Management, Second Edition
by Quentin W. Fleming and Joel M. Koppelman

Effective Project Management: How to Plan, Manage, and Deliver Projects on Time and Within Budget
by Robert K. Wysocki, et al.

A Guide to the Project Management Body of Knowledge (PMBOK® Guide)
by the PMI Standards Committee

Global Literacies: Lessons on Business Leadership and National Cultures
by Robert Rosen (Editor), Patricia Digh and Carl Phillips

Human Resource Skills for the Project Manager
by Vijay K. Verma

The New Project Management
by J. Davidson Frame

Organizing Projects for Success
by Vijay K. Verma

Principles of Project Management
by John Adams, et al.

Project & Program Risk Management
by R. Max Wideman, Editor

Project Management Casebook
Edited by David I. Cleland, et al.

Project Management Experience and Knowledge Self-Assessment Manual
by Project Management Institute

Project Management: A Managerial Approach, Fourth Edition
by Jack R. Meredith and Samuel J. Mantel Jr.

Project Management: A Systems Approach to Planning, Scheduling, and Controlling, Seventh Edition
by Harold Kerzner

A GUIDE TO THE PROJECT MANAGEMENT BODY OF KNOWLEDGE (PMBOK® GUIDE)

The basic management reference for everyone who works on projects. Serves as a tool for learning about the generally accepted knowledge and practices of the profession. As "management by projects" becomes more and more a recommended business practice worldwide, the *PMBOK® Guide* becomes an essential source of information that should be on every manager's bookshelf. Available in hardcover or paperback, the *PMBOK® Guide* is an official standards document of the Project Management Institute.
ISBN: 1-880410-12-5 (paperback), ISBN: 1-880410-13-3 (hardcover)

MANAGING PROJECTS STEP-BY-STEP™

Follow the steps, standards, and procedures used and proven by thousands of professional project managers and leading corporations. This interactive multimedia CD-ROM, based on PMI's *PMBOK® Guide,* will enable you to customize, standardize, and distribute your project plan standards, procedures, and methodology across your entire organization. Multimedia illustrations using 3-D animations and audio make this perfect for both self-paced training or for use by a facilitator.

PMBOK Q&A

Use this handy pocket-sized question-and-answer study guide to learn more about the key themes and concepts presented in PMI's international standard, *PMBOK® Guide.* More than 160 multiple-choice questions with answers (referenced to the *PMBOK® Guide*) help you with the breadth of knowledge needed to understand key project management concepts.
ISBN: 1-880410-21-4 (paperback)

PMI PROCEEDINGS LIBRARY CD-ROM

This interactive guide to PMI's annual Seminars & Symposium proceedings offers a powerful new option to the traditional methods of document storage and retrieval, research, training, and technical writing. Contains complete paper presentations from PMI '92–PMI '97 with full-text search capability, convenient onscreen readability, and PC/Mac compatibility.

PMI PUBLICATIONS LIBRARY CD-ROM

Using state-of-the-art technology, PMI offers complete articles and information from its major publications on one CD-ROM, including *PM Network* (1990–97), *Project Management Journal* (1990–97), and *A Guide to the Project Management Body of Knowledge.* Offers full-text search capability and indexing by *PMBOK® Guide* knowledge areas. Electronic indexing schemes and sophisticated search engines help to quickly find and retrieve articles that are relevant to your topic or research area.

ALSO AVAILABLE FROM PMI

Project Management for Managers
Mihály Görög, Nigel J. Smith
ISBN: 1-880410-54-0 (paperback)

Project Leadership: From Theory to Practice
Jeffery K. Pinto, Peg Thoms, Jeffrey Trailer, Todd Palmer,
Michele Govekar
ISBN: 1-880410-10-9 (paperback)

Annotated Bibliography of Project and Team Management
David I. Cleland, Gary Rafe, Jeffrey Mosher
ISBN: 1-880410-47-8 (paperback)
ISBN: 1-880410-57-5 (CD-ROM)

How to Turn Computer Problems into Competitive Advantage
Tom Ingram
ISBN: 1-880410-08-7 (paperback)

Achieving the Promise of Information Technology
Ralph B. Sackman
ISBN: 1-880410-03-6 (paperback)

Leadership Skills for Project Managers
Editors' Choice Series
Edited by Jeffery K. Pinto, Jeffrey W. Trailer
ISBN: 1-880410-49-4 (paperback)

The Virtual Edge
Margery Mayer
ISBN: 1-880410-16-8 (paperback)

The ABCs of DPC
Edited by PMI's Design-Procurement-Construction
Specific Interest Group
ISBN: 1-880410-07-9 (paperback)

Project Management Casebook
Edited by David I. Cleland, Karen M. Bursic,
Richard Puerzer, A. Yaroslav Vlasak
ISBN: 1-880410-45-1 (paperback)

Project Management Casebook Instructor's Manual
Edited by David I. Cleland, Karen M. Bursic,
Richard Puerzer, A. Yaroslav Vlasak
ISBN: 1-880410-18-4 (paperback)

The PMI Book of Project Management Forms
ISBN: 1-880410-31-1 (paperback)
ISBN: 1-880410-50-8 (diskette version)

Principles of Project Management
John Adams et al.
ISBN: 1-880410-30-3 (paperback)

Organizing Projects for Success
Human Aspects of Project Management Series, Volume 1
Vijay K. Verma
ISBN: 1-880410-40-0 (paperback)

Human Resource Skills for the Project Manager
Human Aspects of Project Management Series, Volume 2
Vijay K. Verma
ISBN: 1-880410-41-9 (paperback)

Managing the Project Team
Human Aspects of Project Management Series, Volume 3
Vijay K. Verma
ISBN: 1-880410-42-7 (paperback)

Value Management Practice
Michel Thiry
ISBN: 1-880410-14-1 (paperback)

Decision Analysis in Projects
John R. Schuyler
ISBN: 1-880410-39-7 (paperback)

The World's Greatest Project
Russell W. Darnall
ISBN: 1-880410-46-X (paperback)

Power & Politics in Project Management
Jeffrey K. Pinto
ISBN: 1-880410-43-5 (paperback)

Best Practices of Project Management Groups in Large Functional Organizations
Frank Toney, Ray Powers
ISBN: 1-880410-05-2 (paperback)

Project Management in Russia
Vladimir I. Voropajev
ISBN: 1-880410-02-8 (paperback)

A Framework for Project and Program Management Integration
R. Max Wideman
ISBN: 1-880410-01-X (paperback)

Quality Management for Projects & Programs
Lewis R. Ireland
ISBN: 1-880410-11-7 (paperback)

Project & Program Risk Management
Edited by R. Max Wideman
ISBN: 1-880410-06-0 (paperback)

Order online at
www.pmibookstore.org

Book Ordering Information

Phone: 412.741.6206
Fax: 412.741.0609
Email: pmiorders@abdintl.com

Mail: PMI Publications Fulfillment Center
PO Box 1020
Sewickley, Pennsylvania 15143-1020 USA

LP437 . 183